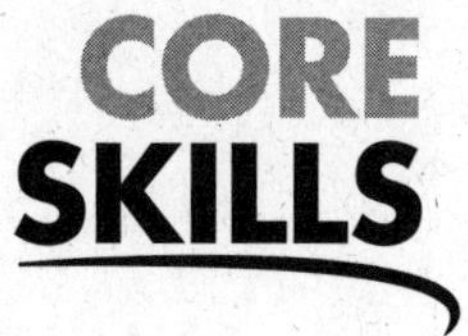

n

Harcourt

Spelling

Grade 2

Printed in the U.S.A.

ISBN 978-0-544-26779-4

1 2 3 4 5 6 7 8 9 10 0982 22 21 20 19 18 17 16 15 14 13

4500438417 A B C D E F G

Core Skills Spelling

Grade 2

Introduction

Core Skills Spelling is a research-based, systematic spelling program developed to help students master spelling. The program is based on three critical goals for students:

- to learn to spell common spelling patterns and troublesome words
- to learn strategies related to sounds and spelling patterns
- to link spelling and meaning

Each book in the *Core Skills Spelling* program is composed of 30 skill lessons. The majority of skill lessons in this program focus on spellings of vowel sounds. Other skill lessons focus on word structure and content-area words.

Key features of this book include:

- study steps that focus learning,
- a spelling table that contains common spellings for consonant and vowel sounds,
- lessons that build competency and provide visual reinforcement,
- word study that expands vocabulary and meaning,
- engaging vocabulary and context activities that encourage students to explore word meanings and use words in meaningful contexts, and
- challenge sections that present opportunities to enrich vocabulary and extend spelling skills..

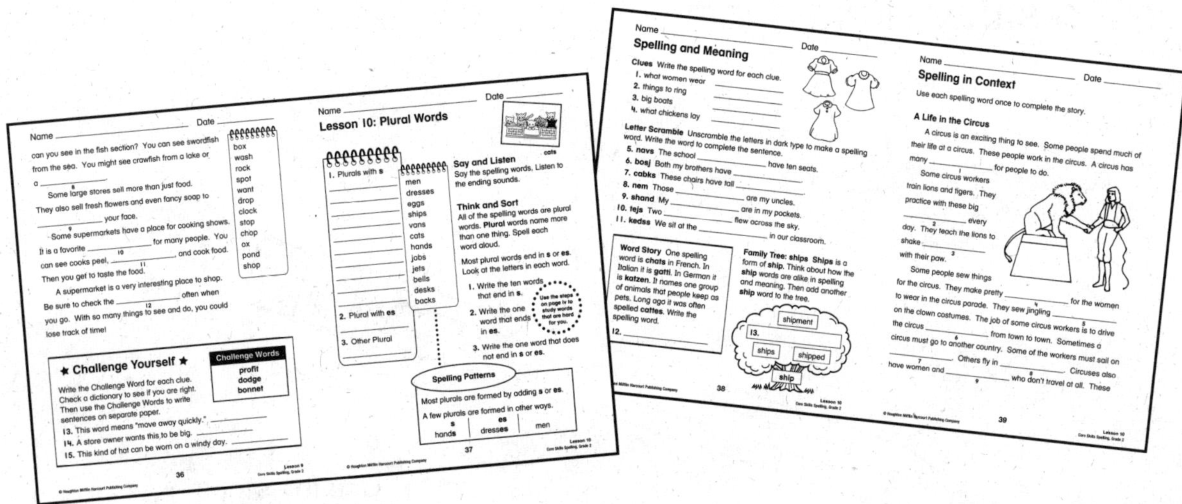

Name ________ Date ________

can you see in the fish section? You can see swordfish from the sea. You might see crawfish from a lake or a ________.[8]

Some large stores sell more than just food. They also sell fresh flowers and even fancy soap to ________[9] your face.

Some supermarkets have a place for cooking shows. It is a favorite ________[10] for many people. You can see cooks peel, ________[11], and cook food. Then you get to taste the food.

A supermarket is a very interesting place to shop. Be sure to check the ________[12] often when you go. With so many things to see and do, you could lose track of time!

box, wash, rock, spot, want, drop, clock, stop, chop, ox, pond, shop

★ Challenge Yourself ★

Write the Challenge Word for each clue. Check a dictionary to see if you are right. Then use the Challenge Words to write sentences on separate paper.

Challenge Words: profit, dodge, bonnet

13. This word means "move away quickly." ________
14. A store owner wants this to be big. ________
15. This kind of hat can be worn on a windy day. ________

© Houghton Mifflin Harcourt Publishing Company 36 Lesson 9 Core Skills Spelling, Grade 2

Name ________ Date ________

Lesson 10: Plural Words

cats

1. Plurals with **s**
2. Plural with **es**
3. Other Plural

men, dresses, eggs, ships, vans, cats, hands, jobs, jets, bells, desks, backs

Say and Listen
Say the spelling words. Listen to the ending sounds.

Think and Sort
All of the spelling words are plural words. **Plural** words name more than one thing. Spell each word aloud.

Most plural words end in **s** or **es**. Look at the letters in each word.

1. Write the ten words that end in **s**.
2. Write the one word that ends in **es**.
3. Write the one word that does not end in **s** or **es**.

Use the steps on page iv to study words that are hard for you.

Spelling Patterns

Most plurals are formed by adding **s** or **es**.
A few plurals are formed in other ways.

s	es	
hand**s**	dress**es**	men

© Houghton Mifflin Harcourt Publishing Company 37 Lesson 10 Core Skills Spelling, Grade 2

Name ________ Date ________

Spelling and Meaning

Clues Write the spelling word for each clue.
1. what women wear ________
2. things to ring ________
3. big boats ________
4. what chickens lay ________

Letter Scramble Unscramble the letters in dark type to make a spelling word. Write the word to complete the sentence.
5. **navs** The school ________ have ten seats.
6. **bosj** Both my brothers have ________.
7. **cabks** These chairs have tall ________.
8. **nem** Those ________ are my uncles.
9. **shand** My ________ are in my pockets.
10. **tejs** Two ________ flew across the sky.
11. **kedss** We sit at the ________ in our classroom.

Word Story One spelling word is **chats** in French. In Italian it is **gatti**. In German it is **katzen**. It names one group of animals that people keep as pets. Long ago it was often spelled **cattes**. Write the spelling word.
12. ________

Family Tree: ships **Ships** is a form of **ship**. Think about how the **ship** words are alike in spelling and meaning. Then add another **ship** word to the tree.

shipment, 13. ________, ships, shipped, ship

© Houghton Mifflin Harcourt Publishing Company 38 Lesson 10 Core Skills Spelling, Grade 2

Name ________ Date ________

Spelling in Context

Use each spelling word once to complete the story.

A Life in the Circus

A circus is an exciting thing to see. Some people spend much of their life at a circus. These people work in the circus. A circus has many ________[1] for people to do.

Some circus workers train lions and tigers. They practice with these big ________[2] every day. They teach the lions to shake ________[3] with their paw.

Some people sew things for the circus. They make pretty ________[4] for the women to wear in the circus parade. They sew jingling ________[5] on the clown costumes. The job of some circus workers is to drive the circus ________[6] from town to town. Sometimes a circus must go to another country. Some of the workers must sail on ________[7]. Others fly in ________[8]. Circuses also have women and ________[9] who don't travel at all. These

© Houghton Mifflin Harcourt Publishing Company 39 Lesson 10 Core Skills Spelling, Grade 2

Study Steps to Learn a Word

1. **Say** the word. What consonant sounds do you hear? What vowel sounds do you hear? How many syllables do you hear?

2. **Look** at the letters in the word. Think about how each sound is spelled. Find any spelling patterns or parts that you know. Close your eyes. Picture the word in your mind.

3. **Spell** the word aloud.

4. **Write** the word. Say each letter as you write it.

5. **Check** the spelling. If you did not spell the word correctly, use the study steps again.

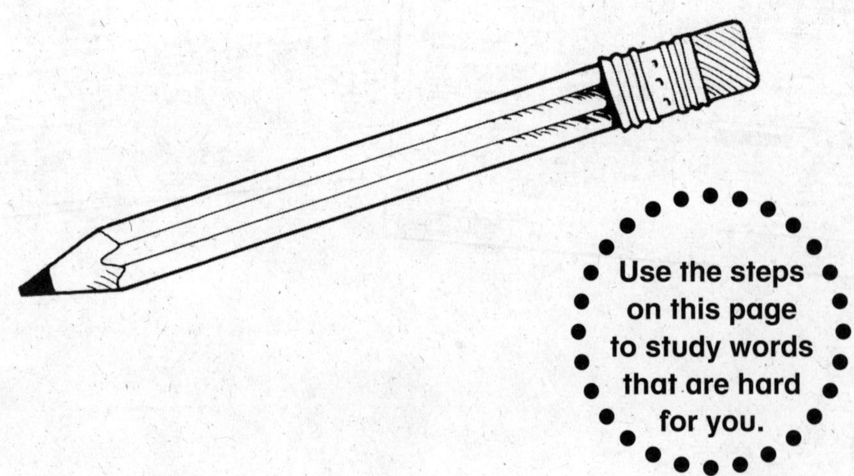

Spelling Table

Consonants

Sound	Example Words	Spellings
b	big	b
ch	child, catch	ch tch
d	day, add	d dd
f	fast, off	f ff
g	get, egg	g gg
h	hand, who	h wh
j	jog, sponge	j g
k	can, keep, school, sick	c k ch ck
ks	six	x
kw	quit	qu
l	look, all	l ll
m	made, swimming, numb	m mm mb
n	not, running, knock	n nn kn
ng	thank, ring	n ng
p	pet, dropped	p pp
r	run, writer	r wr
s	sat, dress, city	s ss c
sh	she	sh
t	ten, matter	t tt
th	that, thing	th
v	have, of	v f
w	went, whale, one	w wh o
y	you	y
z	zoo, blizzard, says	z zz s

Vowels

Sound	Example Words	Spellings
short a	cat, have	a a_e
long a	baby, take, play, nail, eight, they	a a_e ay ai eigh ey
ah	father, star	a
short e	red, tread, many, said, says	e ea a ai ay
long e	he, eat, tree, people, belief, very	e ea ee eo ie y
short i	is, give	i i_e
long i	find, ride, pie, high my, eye	i i_e ie igh y eye
short o	on, want	o a
long o	so, nose, road, boulder, snow	o o_e oa ou ow
oi	boy	oy
aw	off, call, haul, saw	o a au aw
o	corn, store, door, four	o o_e oo ou
long oo	zoo, blue, new, do, you	oo ue ew o ou
short oo	good, could, pull	oo ou u
ow	out, owl	ou ow
short u	run, brother	u o

Commonly Misspelled Words

about	family	name	their
above	favorite	nice	then
across	friend	now	there
again	friends	once	they
a lot	get	one	though
am	getting	our	time
and	girl	out	today
another	goes	outside	too
are	guess	party	two
because	have	people	upon
been	hear	play	very
before	her	please	want
beginning	here	pretty	was
bought	him	read	went
boy	his	really	were
buy	house	right	when
can	in	said	where
came	into	saw	white
children	know	scared	with
color	like	school	would
come	little	sent	write
didn't	made	some	writing
does	make	store	wrote
don't	me	swimming	your
every	my	teacher	you're

Name ______________________ Date ______________

Lesson 1: Words with Short *a*

cat

1. Beginning Short a

____

____

____

____

____

2. Middle Short a

____

____

____

____

____

____

____

van
an
after
flat
hand
cat
and
has
am
than
add
man

Say and Listen

Say each spelling word. Listen for the vowel sound you hear in **van**.

Think and Sort

The vowel sound in **van** is called short **a**. All of the spelling words have the short **a** sound. It is spelled **a**. Spell each word aloud.

Look at the letters in each word. Is the short **a** at the beginning or in the middle of the word?

1. Write the five spelling words that have short **a** at the beginning.

Use the steps on page iv to study words that are hard for you.

2. Write the seven spelling words that have short **a** in the middle.

Spelling Patterns

The short **a** sound can be spelled **a**.

add	v**a**n

Name ______________________________ Date ____________

Spelling and Meaning

Clues Write the spelling word for each clue.

1. what you can do with numbers ____________
2. part of an arm ____________
3. pet that meows ____________
4. the opposite of **before** ____________
5. what a boy grows up to be ____________

Letter Scramble Unscramble the letters in dark type to make a spelling word. Write the word to complete the sentence.

6. **na** I ate ______________ apple.
7. **hant** His friend is older ______________ he is.
8. **ahs** Rita is not here because she ______________ a cold.
9. **ma** You are tall, but I ______________ short.
10. **latf** The top of a table is ______________.
11. **dna** Sam likes blue ______________ purple.

Word Story One spelling word comes from the word **caravan**. A long time ago, a **caravan** was a covered carriage or cart. Write the spelling word that comes from **caravan**.

12. ______________

Family Tree: hand Think about how the **hand** words are alike in spelling and meaning. Then add another **hand** word to the tree.

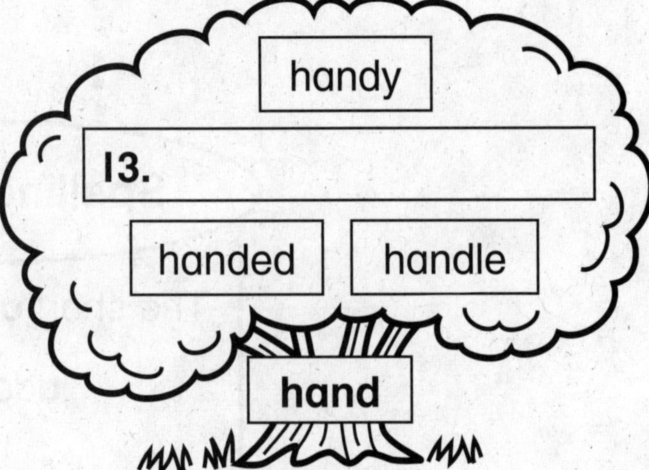

Name ______________________ Date ____________

Spelling in Context

Use each spelling word once to complete the selection.

To the Rescue!

Sometimes wild animals need help. Storms destroy their home. They get sick or hurt. Their babies get lost. Wildlife rescue groups can help these animals. These groups take care of animals in special parks just for wildlife. They do even more ________ (1) care for the animals, though. They also return some of them to their natural home ________ (2) the animals are well or old enough.

What kinds of animals do wildlife rescue groups help? They help any animal in need. Most wildlife parks have raccoons ________ (3) birds. Some even have bobcats. A bobcat is a wild ________ (4).

Wildlife parks have trees that animals can climb. The parks also have ________ (5) places where animals can walk and run.

Name ______________________ Date ____________

What should you do if you see ____________ (6) animal in trouble? Do not try to pick up the animal. If you do, the animal may bite your ____________ (7). Instead, call a wildlife rescue group. Your phone book ____________ (8) names of rescue groups you can call. A ____________ (9) or a woman will come to help. The worker will put the animal in a truck or a ____________ (10) and take it to a wildlife park. People at the park will give the animal the care it needs. You can tell them to ____________ (11) your name to their list of helpers.

Are you ready to become a rescue helper? If you are, say, "I ____________ (12)!"

van
an
after
flat
hand
cat
and
has
am
than
add
man

★ Challenge Yourself ★

What do you think each Challenge Word means? Check a dictionary to see if you are right. Then use the Challenge Words to write sentences on separate paper.

Challenge Words

active
blank
habit

13. Monkeys and kangaroos are **active** animals.

14. Erase your answer and leave the box **blank**.

15. Brushing your teeth is a good **habit**.

Name ______________________ Date __________

Lesson 2: More Words with Short *a*

catch

1. Beginning Short **a**

____

2. Middle Short **a**

____
____
____
____
____
____
____
____
____
____
____

catch
fast
matter
have
land
that
back
last
thank
ask
sang
black

Say and Listen

Say each spelling word. Listen for the short **a** sound.

Think and Sort

All of the spelling words have the short **a** sound. It is spelled **a**. Spell each word aloud.

Look at the letters in each spelling word. Is the short **a** at the beginning or in the middle of the word?

1. Write the one word that has short **a** at the beginning.

Use the steps on page iv to study words that are hard for you.

2. Write the eleven words that have short **a** in the middle. One word has an **e** at the end, but the **e** is silent. Circle the word.

Spelling Patterns

The short **a** sound can be spelled **a**.

ask	b**a**ck	h**a**ve

Name ______________________ Date ____________

Spelling and Meaning

Word Groups Write the spelling word that belongs in each group.

1. danced, acted, ____________
2. sea, sky, ____________
3. orange, yellow, ____________
4. throw, hit, ____________
5. quick, swift, ____________
6. had, has, ____________

Rhymes Write the spelling word that completes each sentence and rhymes with the underlined word.

7. Why did Dee ____________ for that silly <u>mask</u>?
8. Hector wanted to ____________ me for the piggy <u>bank</u>.
9. What is the ____________ with the pancake <u>batter</u>?
10. Ming ran around the <u>track</u> and ____________ home.
11. What is the name of ____________ <u>cat</u>?

Word Story Long ago one of the spelling words was spelled **latost**. It meant "latest." Now it means "coming at the end." It has a different spelling, too. Write the word.

12. ____________

Family Tree: thank Think about how the **thank** words are alike in spelling and meaning. Then add another **thank** word to the tree.

Name ______________________________ Date ______________

Spelling in Context

Use each spelling word once to complete the story.

The Violin Lesson

Ann's mother said she would be ______________ (1) at two o'clock. Ann picked up her violin case and got out of the car. "It doesn't ______________ (2) if you're late," she said. "I have a lot of practicing to do."

Ann watched her mother drive off. It was a beautiful spring day. Children were playing ______________ (3) and tag at the park. A bird ______________ (4) above her head. Ann watched the bird ______________ (5) near the feet of a girl. The girl was older than Ann. She was carrying a ______________ (6) violin case.

"Hi!" Ann called. "I ______________ (7) never seen you here before. My name is Ann. I've been taking lessons from Mr. Crabbe each week for the ______________ (8) six months."

"I start today," the tall girl said.

"Well, let me tell you about Mr. Crabbe. He'll want you to practice a lot! I practice every day. At first I could only play slow songs.

Name ______________________ Date ____________

Now I can even play some really ________
9
ones. I have Mr. Crabbe to ________ for
10
being a good player. He's a very good teacher."

The tall girl smiled. "Do you know who I am?" she asked Ann.

"No, I don't," Ann said. She hadn't thought to ________ the girl's name.
11

"I'm Tina Crabbe. Mr. Crabbe is my grandfather," Tina said. "Thank you for saying ________
12
he's a good teacher."

Ann smiled. She said good-bye and went inside for her lesson with Mr. Crabbe.

- catch
- fast
- matter
- have
- land
- that
- back
- last
- thank
- ask
- sang
- black

★ Challenge Yourself ★

Challenge Words

napkin
craft
cannon

Use a dictionary to answer these questions. Then use the Challenge Words to write sentences on separate paper.

13. Does a potter have a **craft**? ________

14. Do people use a **napkin** to clean their hands after a meal?

____

15. Would you find a **cannon** in your kitchen? ________

Name ____________________ Date __________

Lesson 3: Words with Short *e*

jet

1. e Words

____
____
____
____
____
____
____
____
____
____

2. ay Word

____

3. ai Word

____

ten
when
bed
shelf
jet
yes
said
went
kept
says
next
end

Say and Listen

Say each spelling word. Listen for the vowel sound you hear in **ten**.

Think and Sort

The vowel sound in **ten** is called short **e**. All of the spelling words have the short **e** sound. Spell each word aloud.

Look at the letters in each word. Think about how short **e** is spelled.

1. Write the ten spelling words that have short **e** spelled **e**.
2. Write the one spelling word that has short **e** spelled **ay**.
3. Write the one spelling word that has short **e** spelled **ai**.

Use the steps on page iv to study words that are hard for you.

Spelling Patterns

The short **e** sound can be spelled **e**, **ay**, or **ai**.

e	**ay**	**ai**
ten	says	said

Name ______________________ Date ____________

Spelling and Meaning

Word Math Add and subtract letters and picture names. Write each spelling word.

1. b + [picture] – sl = ______________
2. sh + [picture] = ______________
3. w + [picture] = ______________
4. [picture] – am + et = ______________
5. [picture] – p + d = ______________

Word Groups Write the spelling word that belongs in each group.

6. near, beside, ______________
7. told, asked, ______________
8. saved, stored, ______________
9. eight, nine, ______________
10. no, maybe, ______________
11. tells, asks, ______________

Word Story Long ago one of the spelling words was spelled **wente**. It meant "did go." Its meaning hasn't changed, but its spelling has. Write the spelling that we use today.

12. ______________

Family Tree: end Think about how the **end** words are alike in spelling and meaning. Then add another **end** word to the tree.

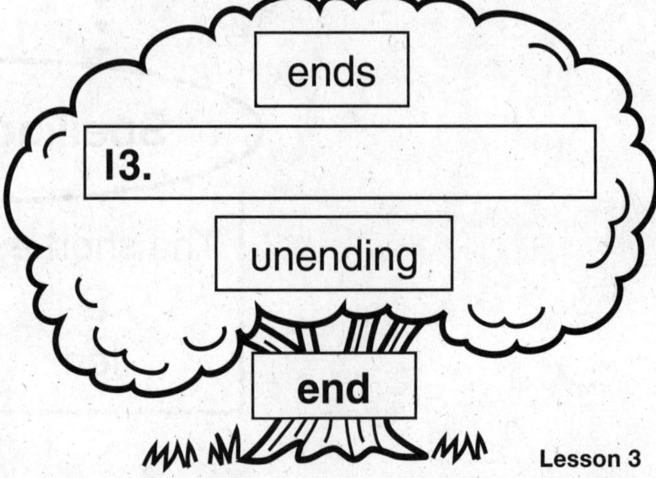

Name ______________________ Date ____________

Spelling in Context

Use each spelling word once to complete the story.

Jet Travel

Long ago travel could take days or weeks. When people needed to go far away, they usually ________ (1) on trains and ships. Over the years, travel ________ (2) getting faster and faster. Today people can fly from one place to another on a ________ (3).

What do you do ________ (4) you travel on a jet? The first thing you do is find your seat. A jet has many rows of seats. Some seats are ________ (5) to windows.

You might need to store things that you have with you. A closed-in ________ (6) hangs above each row of seats. People put things such as coats and small bags on the shelf.

Next put on your seat belt and get ready for the trip. Someone will tell about safety. Listen carefully. What that person ________ (7) is important. In case of an emergency, you will want to remember what the person showed you and ________ (8) to do.

Name ______________________________ Date ____________

You will also hear the pilot speak. The pilot will tell about the weather and the flight.

Someone might ask if you would like something to eat or drink. If you say ______________ (9), you will get a snack or a meal. You might want to rest or sleep. A flight across the sea can last nine or ______________ (10) hours—or more. Many people try to sleep on long trips. The seat leans back. It is almost as if you are lying in a ______________ (11).

At the ______________ (12) of the trip, the pilot will speak again. He or she will tell about the landing. The pilot and crew will also thank you for flying with them. They look forward to seeing you on your next trip!

- ten
- when
- bed
- shelf
- jet
- yes
- said
- went
- kept
- says
- next
- end

★ Challenge Yourself ★

Challenge Words

melon
pedal
method

What do you think each Challenge Word means? Check a dictionary to see if you are right. Then use the Challenge Words to write sentences on separate paper.

13. The best **method** of brushing your teeth is brushing in circles.

14. My favorite fruit at the picnic was the **melon**.

15. My sister's bike needs a new **pedal**.

Name ______________________ Date ____________

Lesson 4: More Words with Short *e*

bell

1. e Words

____

____

____

____

____

____

____

____

____

____

2. a Words

____

____

best
well
any
seven
many
dress
desk
rest
bell
send
help
egg

Say and Listen

Say each spelling word. Listen for the short **e** sound.

Think and Sort

All of the spelling words have the short **e** sound. Spell each word aloud.

Look at the letters in each word. Think about how short **e** is spelled. How many spellings for short **e** do you see?

1. Write the ten spelling words that have short **e** spelled **e**.
2. Write the two spelling words that have short **e** spelled **a**.

Use the steps on page iv to study words that are hard for you.

Spelling Patterns

The short **e** sound can be spelled **e** or **a**.

e	a
desk	any

Name ______________________ Date ______________

Spelling and Meaning

Word Groups Write the spelling word that belongs in each group.

1. five, six, ______________
2. several, lots, ______________
3. table, chair, ______________
4. good, better, ______________
5. one, every, ______________
6. good, fine, ______________

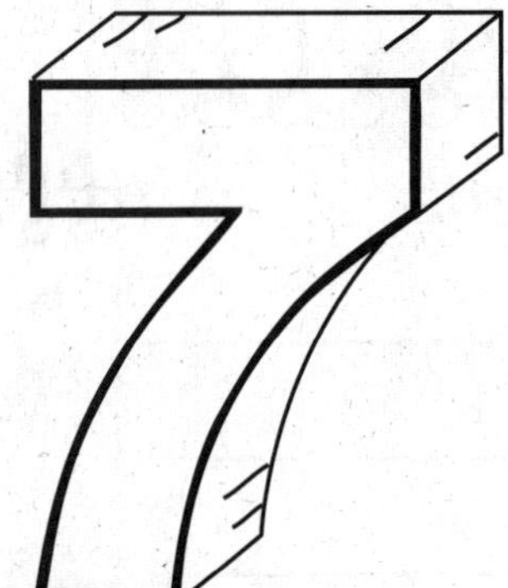

What's Missing? Write the missing spelling word.

7. the chicken and the ______________
8. ring the ______________
9. ______________ an e-mail
10. ______________ when you're tired
11. a woman's ______________

Word Story One of the spelling words comes from an old word that was spelled **hjalpa**. Then the spelling was changed to **helpen**. Write the spelling that we use today.

12. ______________

Family Tree: dress Think about how the **dress** words are alike in spelling and meaning. Then add another **dress** word to the tree.

Name ______________________ Date ____________

Spelling in Context

Use each spelling word once to complete the story.

Meg's Chickens

October 20

Dear Diary,

Today is my birthday. Tonight will be special. My family and I will have a party. We will have birthday cake and ice cream. I will wear my best ______________.
1

School was really special today. Last week Grandpa said he would ______________ me a surprise.
2
He sent me eight eggs to take to class. Everyone wanted to see baby chicks being born. The eggs hatched today. What a surprise that was!

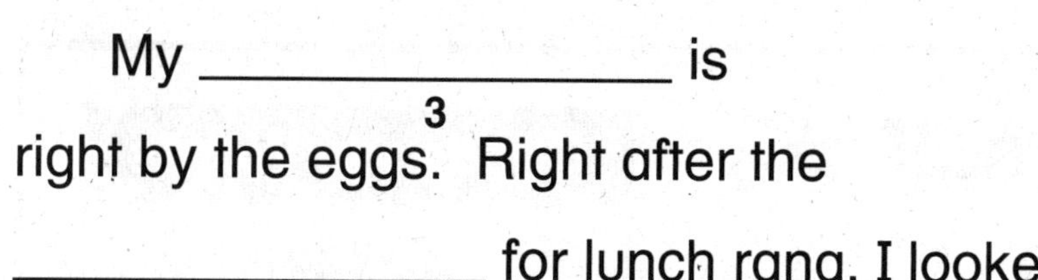

My ______________ is
3
right by the eggs. Right after the ______________ for lunch rang, I looked in
4
the box. I saw that one ______________ was beginning to crack.
5

Everyone ran to see the new chick. One by one, the other ______________ eggs began to crack. Soon we could see all the
6
babies. Then my friend Riley said, "I've never seen ______________
7
chickens like those before!"

Name ______________________ Date __________

"Where did you get the eggs?" my teacher asked.

"My grandfather gave them to me," I said. "He wants to ______ (8) me learn about the animals on his farm."

My teacher laughed. "He likes to play jokes, too," she said. The ______ (9) of the class also laughed. Not ______ (10) things surprise me. But the eight tiny turtles crawling around in the box sure did!

When I left school, all the baby turtles were doing ______ (11). Everyone calls them Meg's chickens. Grandpa gave me the ______ (12) birthday surprise ever!

best
well
any
seven
many
dress
desk
rest
bell
send
help
egg

★ Challenge Yourself ★

Challenge Words
beggar
tread
memory

Decide which Challenge Word fits each clue. Check a dictionary to see if you are right. Then use the Challenge Words to write sentences on separate paper.

13. A good one will help you in school. __________

14. This is someone who begs. __________

15. When you walk on something, you do this. __________

Name ______________________ Date ____________

Lesson 5: People Words

girls

I. Three Letters

____
____
____
____
____
____

2. More Than Three Letters

____
____
____
____
____
____

had
class
him
you
children
boys
our
girls
the
them
her
child

Say and Listen

Say the spelling words. Listen to the sounds in each word.

Think and Sort

Look at the letters in each word. Think about how each sound in the word is spelled. Spell each word aloud.

I. Write the six spelling words that have three letters.

2. Write the six spelling words that have more than three letters.

Use the steps on page iv to study words that are hard for you.

Three Letters	More Than Three Letters
him	boys
	child
	children

Name ______________________ Date __________

Spelling and Meaning

Letter Scramble Unscramble the letters in dark type to make a spelling word. Write the word to complete the sentence.

1. **hte** I saw a baby bird at ______________ park.
2. **reh** That is ______________ new dress.
3. **hmet** The lions have their cubs with ______________.
4. **lascs** My ______________ went to the zoo.
5. **cdlnerhi** Young people are called ______________.
6. **lihdc** The little ______________ had a toy boat.
7. **rou** Four people will fit in ______________ car.

Rhymes Write the spelling word that completes each sentence and rhymes with the underlined word.

8. Do you know what Dad ______________?
9. Those two ______________ have lots of toys.
10. Happy birthday to ______________!
11. Did you see ______________ swim?

Word Story One spelling word comes from the old word **gyrle**. Long ago **gyrle** meant "child." The spelling word names one kind of children. Write the spelling word.

12. ______________

Family Tree: you Think about how the **you** words are alike in spelling and meaning. Then add another **you** word to the tree.

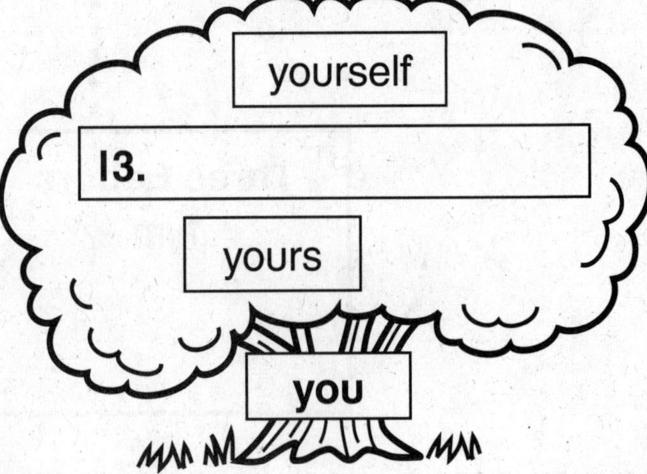

Name ______________________ Date ____________

Spelling in Context

Use each spelling word once to complete the story.

Classrooms of Long Ago

Think about a classroom of today. How many students are in a class? Is each ________ (1) about ________ (2) same age? Today ________ (3) idea of school is a building with many classrooms. All the students in each ________ (4) are close to the same age. It was not this way long ago. Back then ________ (5) of many ages learned together. Students studied in a one-room school. What was school like for ________ (6)?

Students often began the school day with greetings. The ________ (7) often bowed to the teacher. The ________ (8) often curtsied.

Students worked hard at their lessons. They learned to read and to do math. They learned facts and said them over and over. They learned to write neatly. Few students ________ (9) pen and paper.

Name ______________________ Date __________

They wrote on thin, flat stones called slates. They also used pencils made from slate.

At the end of the school day, there were jobs to do. The teacher often asked students to help ______ (10) or ______ (11). Students sometimes wiped the blackboards. They brought in wood for the next day's fire.

Think about schools of long ago. Then think about schools today. Would ______ (12) like to learn in a one-room school? Or would you rather learn in a school of today?

had
class
him
you
children
boys
our
girls
the
them
her
child

★ Challenge Yourself ★

Write the Challenge Word for each clue. Check a dictionary to see if you are right. Then use the Challenge Words to write sentences on separate paper.

Challenge Words
pupil
classmate
buddy

13. This is a word for a close friend. ______

14. This is a student or a part of the eye. ______

15. This names someone in your class. ______

Name ______________________ Date ____________

Lesson 6: Words with Short *i*

ship

1. Three Letters

____
____
____
____

2. Four Letters

____
____
____
____
____
____
____

3. Five Letters

____

big
ship
will
six
fill
hill
this
wind
pick
his
hid
trick

Say and Listen

Say each spelling word. Listen for the vowel sound you hear in **big**.

Think and Sort

The vowel sound you hear in **big** is called short **i**. All the spelling words have the short **i** sound. Spell each word aloud.

Look at the letters in each word. Think about how short **i** is spelled.

1. Write the four spelling words that have three letters.
2. Write the seven spelling words that have four letters.
3. Write the one spelling word that has five letters.

Use the steps on page iv to study words that are hard for you.

Spelling Patterns

The short **i** sound can be spelled **i**.

b**i**g	sh**i**p	tr**i**ck

Name ____________________ Date ____________

Spelling and Meaning

Clues Write the spelling word for each clue.

1. something you can climb ____________

2. a big boat ____________

3. to play a joke on someone ____________

4. the number after five ____________

5. what makes a kite fly ____________

Rhymes Write the spelling word that completes each sentence and rhymes with the underlined word.

6. Jill, please ____________ my glass with water.

7. Luis said that ____________ hat is lost.

8. That wig is too ____________ for my head.

9. Mick will ____________ an apple from that tree.

10. I will miss riding ____________ pony.

11. Marco ____________ still be here tomorrow.

Word Story Long ago the Old English word **hydan** meant "to cover." Over time the spelling changed to **hiden**. One spelling word comes from **hiden**. It means "kept out of sight." Write the spelling word.

12. ____________

Family Tree: fill Think about how the **fill** words are alike in spelling and meaning. Then add another **fill** word to the tree.

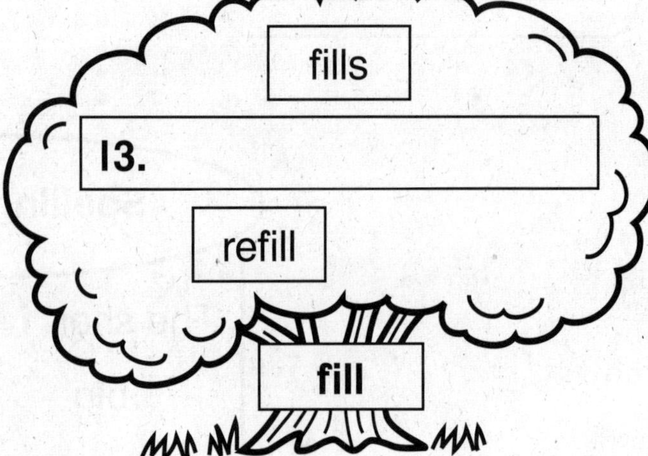

Name ______________________ Date ____________

Spelling in Context

Use each spelling word once to complete the story.

Sail Away

People have used boats since early times. At first people rowed the boats. Then they added sails. The ______(1)______ blew against the sails and made the boats move.

Over time people needed larger boats. These boats could carry more goods and people. A large boat was called a ______(2)______. Most ships were very ______(3)______. Ships needed five or ______(4)______ sails in order to move. Many men worked on a ship. The captain was the leader. One of his jobs was to ______(5)______ the crew that sailed the ship.

Many captains and their crews sailed across the seas. They bought tea, spices, and cloth. Their goal was to ______(6)______ the ship with things they bought. Then they sailed back home and sold the goods. Ships also carried travelers across the ocean. Some people did not have the money to pay the ship's fare. They played a ______(7)______ on the captain. They ______(8)______ on the ship. These people were called stowaways.

Life on a sailing ship was hard. The food was not good. At times there was little fresh water. Great storms often came up suddenly. A wave in a big storm at sea might be as tall as a giant

Name ______________________ Date ____________

______________. People often got sick. When bad
9
things happened, the captain tried to help people. It
was part of ______________ job.
10

After hundreds of years, people stopped using wind to power their ships. Instead they began using steam engines. On ______________ type of ship, people
11
could travel faster.

What kinds of ships do you think people ______________
12
use in the future?

big
ship
will
six
fill
hill
this
wind
pick
his
hid
trick

★ Challenge Yourself ★

Challenge Words
admit
blizzard
glimpse

What do you think each Challenge Word means? Check a dictionary to see if you are right. Then use the Challenge Words to write sentences on separate paper.

13. We got a **glimpse** of the baby deer. Then it was gone.

14. Did she **admit** that she left the door open?

15. School was closed because of the **blizzard**.

Name ______________________ Date ______________

Lesson 7: More Words with Short *i*

fish

1. Four Letters

____

____

____

____

____

____

____

2. Five Letters

____

____

____

3. Six Letters

____

____

ring
give
fish
think
thing
wish
spring
with
live
sister
swim
bring

Say and Listen

Say each spelling word. Listen for the short **i** sound.

Think and Sort

All of the spelling words have the short **i** sound. Spell each word aloud.

Look at the letters in each word. Think about how short **i** is spelled.

1. Write the seven spelling words that have four letters. Two of the words with four letters have an **e** at the end, but the **e** is silent. Circle the words.
2. Write the three spelling words that have five letters.
3. Write the two spelling words that have six letters.

Use the steps on page iv to study words that are hard for you.

Spelling Patterns

The short **i** sound can be spelled **i**.

f**i**sh | g**i**ve | th**i**nk | spr**i**ng

Name ________________________________ Date ______________

Spelling and Meaning

Rhymes Write the spelling word that completes each sentence and rhymes with the underlined word.

1. Birds sing in the ______________.
2. The fried ______________ was on the dish.
3. The king wore a shiny gold ______________.
4. I ______________ Ben is at the skating rink.
5. Please ______________ us some string for the kite.

Word Meanings Write the spelling word for each meaning. Use a dictionary if you need to.

6. to hope for something ______________
7. to hand something over ______________
8. a girl with the same parents as another child ______________
9. an object ______________
10. to move through water ______________
11. having ______________

Word Story Long ago the word that means "to have life" was spelled **lifen**. Over time the spelling changed. Write the spelling word that shows how **lifen** is spelled today.

12. ______________

Family Tree: fish Think about how the **fish** words are alike in spelling and meaning. Then add another **fish** word to the tree.

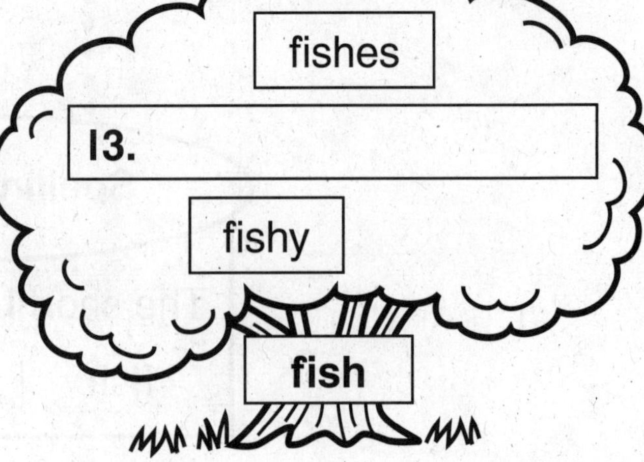

Name ______________________________ Date ______________

Spelling in Context

Use each spelling word once to complete the story.

Spring Changes

Do you ________________ in a place that has long, cold winters?
1
During months of ice and snow, many people ________________ for
2
warmer weather. They would ________________ anything to see
3
flowers budding on trees. They are ready for the long winter to end
and for ________________ to begin. They know that spring will
4
________________ warm, sunny days.
5

Spring brings many changes to land animals. Moles and bats have slept for most of the winter. They have not had a ________________
6
to eat for weeks. They are very hungry. They wake up and look for food.

Many baby animals are born in the spring. Some animal parents take care of their babies. The babies learn to play
________________ each other.
7
It's fun to watch a brother squirrel

Name ______________________ Date __________

chase his ______________. The young animals
8
run and play with other family members, too.

The kind of ______________ called salmon
9
do something special in the spring. They
______________ upstream. They do this to get
10
back to the place where they hatched. There the fish lay their own eggs.

Spring is a happy time. Some people
______________ spring is the best time of the year.
11
They love to hear a robin's song ______________
12
through the air. What do you think?

ring
give
fish
think
thing
wish
spring
with
live
sister
swim
bring

★ Challenge Yourself ★

Challenge Words

bitter
guilt
liberty

What do you think each Challenge Word means? Check a dictionary to see if you are right. Then use the Challenge Words to write sentences on separate paper.

13. This coffee tastes **bitter**.

14. The man admitted his **guilt**.

15. Give the snake its **liberty** after you take it to Show and Tell.

Name ______________________ Date __________

Lesson 8: Words with Short *o*

block

1. o Words

____

____

____

____

____

____

____

____

____

____

2. a Words

____

____

hot
what
dot
not
block
was
job
jog
top
on
hop
got

Say and Listen

Say each spelling word. Listen for the vowel sound you hear in **hot**.

Think and Sort

The vowel sound you hear in **hot** is called short **o**. All the spelling words have the short **o** sound. Spell each word aloud.

Look at the letters in each word. Think about how short **o** is spelled. How many spellings for short **o** do you see?

1. Write the ten spelling words that have short **o** spelled **o**.

Use the steps on page iv to study words that are hard for you.

2. Write the two spelling words that have short **o** spelled **a**.

Spelling Patterns

The short **o** sound can be spelled **o or a**.

o	**a**
dot	was

Name ______________________ Date ______________

Spelling and Meaning

Word Groups Write the spelling word that belongs in each group.

1. run, trot, ______________
2. cold, warm, ______________
3. skip, jump, ______________
4. spot, mark, ______________
5. work, chore, ______________
6. town, street, ______________
7. took, grabbed, ______________

Presto Change-O Change the order of each word in dark type to make a spelling word. Write the spelling word to complete the sentence.

8. **no** Please turn ______________ the light.
9. **ton** Do ______________ touch the oven!
10. **thaw** Please tell me ______________ this is.
11. **saw** Who ______________ at the door?

Word Story One very old word, **tuppaz**, meant "the highest point." The meaning of this word is the same today, but the spelling is different. Write the spelling that we use today.

12. ______________

Family Tree: hop Think about how the **hop** words are alike in spelling and meaning. Then add another **hop** word to the tree.

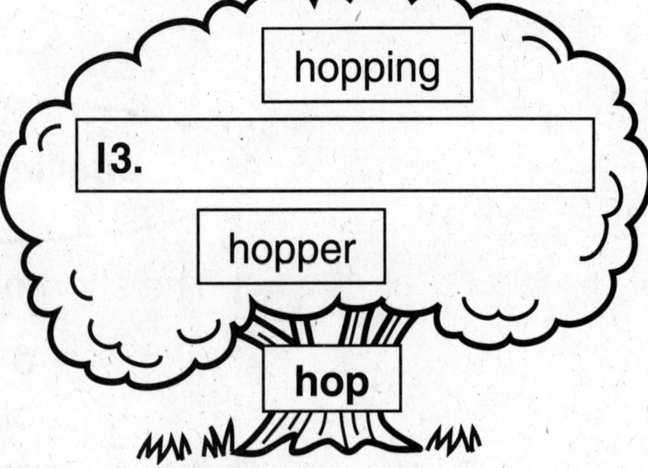

Name ______________________________ Date ____________

Spelling in Context

Use each spelling word once to complete the story.

You Can Make Money

Do you think you are too young to make money? That is ______________ (1) true at all. Are you wondering ______________ (2) you can do to earn money? Here are some ideas.

Walking dogs is a good way to make money. Ask a grownup to go with you when you walk a dog. Then be sure to stay ______________ (3) the sidewalk. Dress for the ______________ (4) and the weather. Wear something that you can move around in easily. Wear warm clothes if it is cold. Wear cool clothing if it is ______________ (5).

Some people will pay you to run errands. Maybe a person ______________ (6) the wrong kind of juice when he or she ______________ (7) out shopping. You could ______________ (8) on your bike or ______________ (9) to the store and exchange it. Try to work for people who live near you or even on the same city ______________ (10). That way, you will never be too far from home.

Name ______________________________ Date ____________

Now are you ready to earn some money? Make a list of things you would like to do. Which is your favorite? Put it at the ______________ of your list. Talk to a grownup about the job you want to try. Then let people know you want work.

11

There is an old saying that you should ______________ every **i** and cross every **t**. That is another way of saying that you should do your best. If you do a good job, you may soon be earning money.

12

Good luck!

hot
what
dot
not
block
was
job
jog
top
on
hop
got

★ Challenge Yourself ★

Challenge Words
lobster **adopt** **monster**

Use a dictionary to answer these questions. Then use the Challenge Words to write sentences on separate paper.

13. Does a **lobster** wear sneakers on its feet? ____________

14. Would a grownup **adopt** another grownup? ____________

15. Do scary movies sometimes have a **monster** in them? ____________

Name ______________________ Date ____________

Lesson 9: More Words with Short *o*

ox

1. o Words

____
____
____
____
____
____
____
____
____
____

2. a Words

____
____

box
wash
rock
spot
want
drop
clock
stop
chop
ox
pond
shop

Say and Listen

Say each spelling word. Listen for the short **o** sound.

Think and Sort

All of the spelling words have the short **o** sound. Spell each word aloud.

Look at the letters in each word. Think about how short **o** is spelled. How many spellings for short **o** do you see?

1. Write the ten spelling words that have short **o** spelled **o**.
2. Write the two spelling words that have short **o** spelled **a**.

Use the steps on page iv to study words that are hard for you.

Spelling Patterns

The short **o** sound can be spelled **o or a**.

o	a
sh**o**p	w**a**nt

Name ______________________ Date ____________

Spelling and Meaning

Word Groups Write the spelling word that belongs in each group.

1. time, watch, ____________
2. wish, need, ____________
3. wait, quit, ____________
4. cut, slice, ____________
5. cow, horse, ____________
6. ocean, lake, ____________
7. clean, scrub, ____________

More Than One Meaning Some words have more than one meaning. Complete each pair of sentences with the correct spelling word.

8. We like to ________________ at that store.
   I buy my skates at a sports ________________.
9. There's a dirty ________________ on my dress.
   Put the book in that ________________.
10. I just felt a ________________ of rain.
    That glass will break if you ________________ it.
11. I found this ________________ in my back yard.
    Will you ________________ the baby?

Word Story One spelling word comes from the Greek word **pyxis**. **Pyxis** was the name of a kind of tree. People used the wood from the tree to make something that could hold things. Write the spelling word that comes from **pyxis**.

12. ________________

Family Tree: want Think about how the **want** words are alike in spelling and meaning. Then add another **want** word to the tree.

Name ______________________________ Date ____________

Spelling in Context

Use each spelling word once to complete the story.

At the Supermarket

People push shopping carts around a big store. They look at shelves as they walk along. They see something they ______________ (1) to buy, and they ______________ (2) their cart. They pick up a can, a bag, or a ______________ (3). Then they ______________ (4) it into the cart. Where are these people? In a supermarket, of course! Many people ______________ (5) for food there each day. You can buy regular foods in a supermarket, such as bread, milk, and eggs. But some supermarkets sell unusual foods, too.

In the produce section, you might see strange vegetables and fruits. You might see fruit shaped like a star. One kind of fruit is brown, hairy, and as hard as a ______________ (6). That fruit is a coconut.

If you visit the meat section, you might find many kinds of meat. You may find buffalo meat or the tail of an ______________ (7). What

Name ______________________________ Date ____________

can you see in the fish section? You can see swordfish from the sea. You might see crawfish from a lake or a ______________.
8

Some large stores sell more than just food. They also sell fresh flowers and even fancy soap to ______________ your face.
9

Some supermarkets have a place for cooking shows. It is a favorite ______________ for many people. You
10
can see cooks peel, ______________, and cook food.
11
Then you get to taste the food.

A supermarket is a very interesting place to shop. Be sure to check the ______________ often when
12
you go. With so many things to see and do, you could lose track of time!

box
wash
rock
spot
want
drop
clock
stop
chop
ox
pond
shop

★ Challenge Yourself ★

Challenge Words

profit
dodge
bonnet

Write the Challenge Word for each clue. Check a dictionary to see if you are right. Then use the Challenge Words to write sentences on separate paper.

13. This word means "move away quickly." ______________

14. A store owner wants this to be big. ______________

15. This kind of hat can be worn on a windy day. ______________

Name ______________________ Date ____________

Lesson 10: Plural Words

cats

1. Plurals with **s**

____
____
____
____
____
____
____
____
____
____

2. Plural with **es**

____

3. Other Plural

____

men
dresses
eggs
ships
vans
cats
hands
jobs
jets
bells
desks
backs

Say and Listen

Say the spelling words. Listen to the ending sounds.

Think and Sort

All of the spelling words are plural words. **Plural** words name more than one thing. Spell each word aloud.

Most plural words end in **s** or **es**. Look at the letters in each word.

1. Write the ten words that end in **s**.

2. Write the one word that ends in **es**.

3. Write the one word that does not end in **s** or **es**.

Use the steps on page iv to study words that are hard for you.

Spelling Patterns

Most plurals are formed by adding **s** or **es**.

A few plurals are formed in other ways.

s	es	
hand**s**	dress**es**	men

Name ______________________ Date ____________

Spelling and Meaning

Clues Write the spelling word for each clue.

1. what women wear ____________
2. things to ring ____________
3. big boats ____________
4. what chickens lay ____________

Letter Scramble Unscramble the letters in dark type to make a spelling word. Write the word to complete the sentence.

5. **navs** The school ____________ have ten seats.
6. **bosj** Both my brothers have ____________.
7. **cabks** These chairs have tall ____________.
8. **nem** Those ____________ are my uncles.
9. **shand** My ____________ are in my pockets.
10. **tejs** Two ____________ flew across the sky.
11. **kedss** We sit at the ____________ in our classroom.

Word Story One spelling word is **chats** in French. In Italian it is **gatti**. In German it is **katzen**. It names one group of animals that people keep as pets. Long ago it was often spelled **cattes**. Write the spelling word.

12. ____________

Family Tree: ships **Ships** is a form of **ship**. Think about how the **ship** words are alike in spelling and meaning. Then add another **ship** word to the tree.

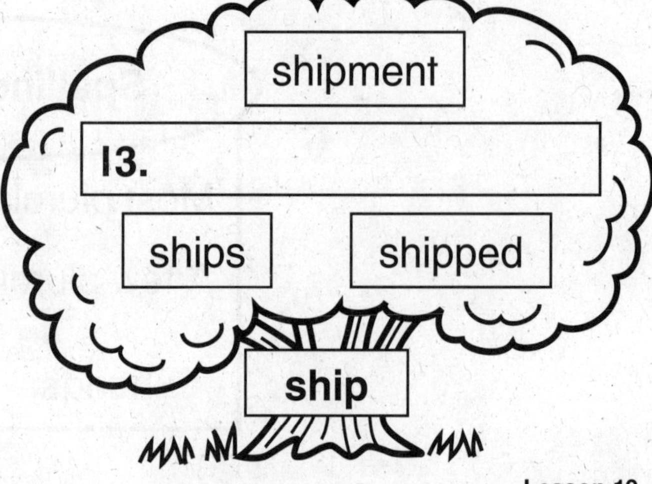

Name ______________________ Date ____________

Spelling in Context

Use each spelling word once to complete the story.

A Life in the Circus

A circus is an exciting thing to see. Some people spend much of their life at a circus. These people work in the circus. A circus has many ______(1)______ for people to do.

Some circus workers train lions and tigers. They practice with these big ______(2)______ every day. They teach the lions to shake ______(3)______ with their paw.

Some people sew things for the circus. They make pretty ______(4)______ for the women to wear in the circus parade. They sew jingling ______(5)______ on the clown costumes. The job of some circus workers is to drive the circus ______(6)______ from town to town. Sometimes a circus must go to another country. Some of the workers must sail on ______(7)______. Others fly in ______(8)______. Circuses also have women and ______(9)______ who don't travel at all. These

Name ______________________________ Date ____________

people sit at ______________ in offices. One of their
10
jobs is to plan where the circus will go next.

Circus people work hard, but they have fun, too. Circus cooks make sure that everyone has a good breakfast. Sometimes clowns do a special juggling act when the cooks' ______________ are turned.
11
On those mornings the circus cooks serve scrambled ______________!
12

- men
- dresses
- eggs
- ships
- vans
- cats
- hands
- jobs
- jets
- bells
- desks
- backs

★ Challenge Yourself ★

Challenge Words

ducklings
batches
recesses

What do you think each Challenge Word means? Check a dictionary to see if you are right. Then use the Challenge Words to write sentences on separate paper.

13. Max made three **batches** of cookies.

14. The **ducklings** swam near their mother.

15. My class gets two **recesses** every day.

Name ______________________ Date ____________

Lesson 11: Words with Short *u*

bus

1. u Words

____
____
____
____
____
____
____
____
____
____
____
____

2. o Words

____
____

sun
under
club
run
bug
from
mud
summer
bus
us
up
cut
of
but

Say and Listen

Say each spelling word. Listen for the vowel sound you hear in **sun**.

Think and Sort

The vowel sound in **sun** is called short **u**. All of the spelling words have the short **u** sound. Spell each word aloud.

Look at the letters in each word. Think about how short **u** is spelled. How many spellings for short **u** do you see?

1. Write the twelve spelling words that have short **u** spelled **u**.
2. Write the two spelling words that have short **u** spelled **o**.

Use the steps on page iv to study words that are hard for you.

Spelling Patterns

The short **u** sound can be spelled **u** or **o**.

u	o
s**u**n	fr**o**m

Name ______________________________ Date ____________

Spelling and Meaning

Antonyms Antonyms are words that have opposite meanings. Write the spelling word that is an antonym of each underlined word.

1. climb <u>down</u> the pole ______________
2. <u>over</u> the trees ______________
3. a letter <u>to</u> you ______________
4. gave <u>them</u> a gift ______________
5. <u>winter</u> days ______________
6. everyone <u>including</u> me ______________
7. <u>walk</u> to the store ______________

Hink Pinks Hink pinks are funny pairs of rhyming words. Read each clue. Write the spelling word that completes each hink pink.

8. a big thing that Gus drives Gus ______________
9. what you can have on a sunny day ______________ fun
10. a place to get your hair trimmed ______________ hut
11. what a baby bear uses for golf cub ______________
12. a mat made for ants and beetles ______________ rug
13. a baby rose made of dirt and water ______________ bud

Word Story One spelling word comes from the Old English word **aef**. **Aef** meant "away from." Today the spelling word means "made from." Write the word.

14. ______________

Family Tree: sun Think about how the **sun** words are alike in spelling and meaning. Then add another **sun** word to the tree.

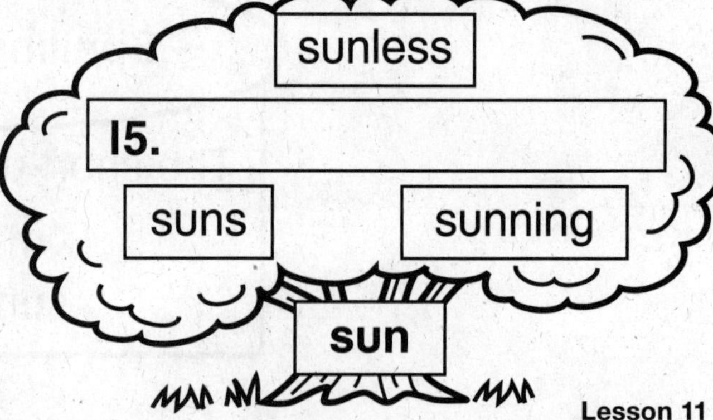

Name ______________________________ Date ____________

Spelling in Context

Use each spelling word once to complete the story.

Day Camp—What Fun!

In the ________________, some boys and girls go to a day camp.
1
Day campers go home at night. That's why their camp is called a day camp!

Families can choose ________________ many day camps. Weeks
2
before summer begins, many newspapers are full ________________
3
ads for day camps. The ads say things like, "Come camp with ________________. You can ride our ________________ to and
4 5
from camp."

What do children do at a day camp? Each camp is different, ________________ a few things
6
are usually the same. Campers spend time outside in the warm summer ________________.
7
They play outdoor games and ________________ races. They
8
also hike ________________ and
9
down hills or along trails. On hikes, campers study plants, animals, and other things they see.

Name ______________________________ Date ______________

They have fun watching a squirrel make a nest or a ______ 10 ______ crawling across a leaf. Some camps give swimming lessons. Campers can learn how to dive and to swim ______ 11 ______ water.

What do campers do when it rains and the ground is covered with ______ 12 ______? They have fun indoors! Campers play board games. They may also have a craft time. During craft time, they paint, ______ 13 ______, and paste. Some day camps have a computer ______ 14 ______ for the campers, too.

Go to a day camp! You can make new friends and have a great time, too!

sun
under
club
run
bug
from
mud
summer
bus
us
up
cut
of
but

★ Challenge Yourself ★

Challenge Words

numb
adjust
buckle

What do you think each Challenge Word means? Check a dictionary to see if you are right. Then use the Challenge Words to write sentences on separate paper.

15. Walking in the snow made my feet **numb**.

16. Please **adjust** the sound on your radio.

17. **Buckle** your seat belt before the car starts.

Name ______________________ Date __________

Lesson 12: More Words with Short *u*

skunk

1. u Words

____
____
____
____
____
____
____
____

2. o Words

____
____
____
____
____
____

just
brother
jump
such
come
love
skunk
much
truck
mother
lunch
one
other
fun

Say and Listen

Say each spelling word. Listen for the short **u** sound.

Think and Sort

All of the spelling words have the short **u** sound. Spell each word aloud.

Look at the letters in each word. Think about how short **u** is spelled.

1. Write the eight spelling words that have short **u** spelled **u**.

Use the steps on page iv to study words that are hard for you.

2. Write the six spelling words that have short **u** spelled **o**. Circle the three words that have a silent **e** at the end.

Spelling Patterns

The short **u** sound can be spelled **u** or **o**.

u	o
j**u**st	c**o**me

Name ______________________ Date ____________

Spelling and Meaning

Word Meanings Write the spelling word for each meaning. Use a dictionary if you need to.

1. to like a lot ________________
2. a lot ________________
3. exactly ________________
4. very ________________
5. a good time ________________
6. different ________________

Partner Words Complete each sentence. Write the spelling word that goes with the underlined word.

7. The cats go out in the morning and ________________ in at night.
8. A rabbit can hop. A frog can ________________.
9. The girl is a sister. The boy is a ________________.
10. A father is a man. A ________________ is a woman.
11. We eat ________________ at noon and dinner at six.
12. I have ________________ nose and two eyes.
13. Will we ride in a ________________ or fly in a plane?

Word Story Native Americans call one animal a **segonku**. It has black and white fur and a bushy tail. The settlers couldn't say the Native American name. Write the spelling word that names the animal now.

14. ________________

Family Tree: jump Think about how the **jump** words are alike in spelling and meaning. Then add another **jump** word to the tree.

Name ______________________ Date ____________

Spelling in Context

Use each spelling word once to complete the story.

A Pet of Our Own

Mom had tried to grow a vegetable garden for years. It was ______(1) harder than you might think. That was because of our neighbor, Mr. Bonzo. He had rabbits. Those rabbits made ______(2) a mess in our garden! They ate the peas and ______(3) vegetables for ______(4). They would leap and ______(5) on the lettuce. They slept on the string beans.

Sometimes my ______(6) tried to talk to Mr. Bonzo about his rabbits. He said, "I ______(7) to watch my rabbits play in your garden. It must make you happy to see them having ______(8)."

Rabbits having fun in her garden did not make Mom a bit happy. "I ______(9) don't know what to do," she said. Then ______(10) day she got an idea.

Name ______________________ Date ____________

"You kids ______________ with me," she said to
11
us. "It's time you had a pet of your own." We hopped in the ______________ and headed for town.
12

My younger ______________, Sammy, and I were
13
excited. "May we get a dog?" I asked.

"We need something fiercer than a dog," said Mom.

"A tiger?" asked Sammy.

"No, smaller than a tiger," said Mom.

"A snake?" I asked in a brave voice.

"No, I don't like snakes," said Mom.

We bought the best pet that the store had. And now we never have any rabbits in our garden. What did we come home with? We got a ______________!
14

- just
- brother
- jump
- such
- come
- love
- skunk
- much
- truck
- mother
- lunch
- one
- other
- fun

★ Challenge Yourself ★

Challenge Words

insult
blush
sponge

What do you think each Challenge Word means? Check a dictionary to see if you are right. Then use the Challenge Words to write sentences on separate paper.

15. It's an **insult** to call someone a skunk.

16. I began to **blush** when I saw the gum in my hair.

17. Wash the sink with a **sponge**.

Name ______________________ Date __________

Lesson 13: Words with Long *a*

whale

1. a-consonant-e Words

____
____
____
____
____
____
____
____

2. ay Words

____
____
____
____
____

3. a Word

____

game
baby
today
came
play
bake
whale
ate
name
say
brave
stay
maybe
gave

Say and Listen

Say each spelling word. Listen for the vowel sound you hear in **game**.

Think and Sort

The vowel sound in **game** is called long **a**. All of the spelling words have the long **a** sound. Spell each word aloud.

Look at the letters in each word. Think about how long **a** is spelled.

1. Write the eight words with long **a** spelled **a**-consonant-**e**.
2. Write the five words with long **a** spelled **ay**.
3. Write the one word with long **a** spelled **a**.

Use the steps on page iv to study words that are hard for you.

Spelling Patterns

The long **a** sound can be spelled **a**-consonant-**e**, **ay**, or **a**.

a-consonant-**e**	**ay**	**a**
game	stay	baby

Name ______________________ Date ____________

Spelling and Meaning

Synonyms Synonyms are words that have the same meaning. Write the spelling word that is a synonym for each word below.

1. cook ______________
2. fearless ______________
3. speak ______________
4. perhaps ______________
5. wait ______________

Word Meanings Write the spelling word for each meaning. Use a dictionary if you need to.

6. to have fun ______________
7. this day ______________
8. contest played with rules ______________
9. handed over ______________
10. what a person or thing is called ______________
11. swallowed food ______________
12. a young child ______________
13. moved towards ______________

Word Story Long ago English sailors called one animal a **hwael**. It is the biggest sea animal of all. Write the spelling that we use today to name this animal.

14. ______________

Family Tree: play Think about how the **play** words are alike in spelling and meaning. Then add another **play** word to the tree.

Name ______________________ Date ____________

Spelling in Context

Use each spelling word once to complete the story.

Alex Tate's Big Day

_______________ was a very special day for Alex Tate and his
1
fans. It was his birthday. He was playing in a very exciting football _______________. The stands were packed with people shouting out
2
his _______________. Alex's fans could not _______________ in
3 4
their seats.

Alex was ready to _______________
5
when the game began. Right away he raced to a touchdown for the Colts. He ended the game with a touchdown, too. The rest of his team _______________ a loud cheer. This
6
_______________ player had won the game
7
on his birthday!

Three cooks had taken the time to _______________ a cake as big as a
8
_______________. At the end of the
9
game, the fans _______________ onto the
10
field. Everyone sang to Alex. They all _______________ a piece of the big cake.
11

Name ________________________________ Date ______________

The other boys on Alex's team ____________ (12) that he thinks about football all the time. "I've loved the game ever since I was a ____________ (13)," says Alex. ____________ (14) his love for the game is what makes him so good!

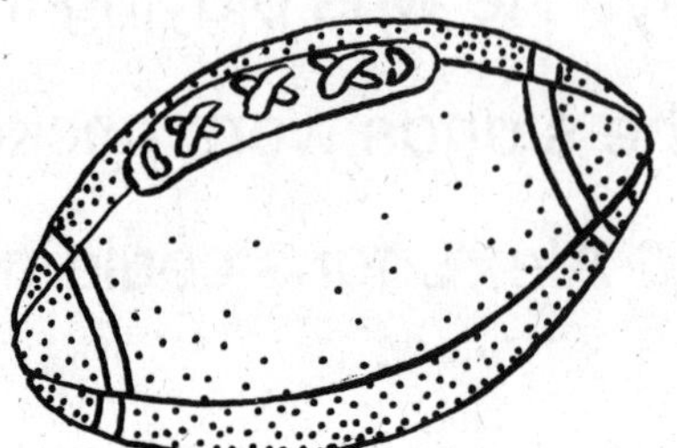

- game
- baby
- today
- came
- play
- bake
- whale
- ate
- name
- say
- brave
- stay
- maybe
- gave

★ Challenge Yourself ★

Challenge Words
delay
bacon
fade

Write the Challenge Word for each clue. Check a dictionary to see if you are right. Then use separate paper to write sentences. Show that you understand the meaning of each Challenge Word.

15. Many people eat this with eggs and toast. ____________

16. Jeans do this after many washings. ____________

17. If you put something off until later, you do this. ____________

Name ______________________ Date ______________

Lesson 14: More Words with Long *a*

train

1. ai Words

____
____
____
____
____
____
____
____
____
____
____
____

2. ei Word

____

3. ey Word

____

chain
gain
eight
tail
paint
nail
pail
they
snail
rain
wait
mail
train
sail

Say and Listen

Say each spelling word. Listen for the long **a** sound.

Think and Sort

All of the spelling words have the long **a** sound. Spell each word aloud.

Look at the letters in each word. Think about how long **a** is spelled. How many spellings for long **a** do you see?

1. Write the twelve spelling words that have long **a** spelled **ai.**
2. Write the one spelling word that has long **a** spelled **ei**.
3. Write the one spelling word that has long **a** spelled **ey**.

Use the steps on page iv to study words that are hard for you.

Spelling Patterns

The long **a** sound can be spelled **ai**, **ei**, or **ey**.

ai	**ei**	**ey**
p**ai**l	**ei**ght	th**ey**

Name ______________________________ Date ____________

Spelling and Meaning

Word Groups Write the spelling word that belongs in each group.

1. wind, snow, ____________
2. boat, plane, ____________
3. hammer, saw, ____________
4. grow, add, ____________
5. draw, color, ____________
6. turtle, worm, ____________
7. he, she, ____________
8. leash, rope, ____________

Homophones Homophones are words that sound the same but have different spellings and meanings. Complete each sentence by writing the spelling word that is a homophone for the underlined word.

9. The ________________ for your boat is on sale.
10. He turned pale when he dropped the ________________.
11. Jesse ate breakfast at ________________.
12. I had to ________________ for him to lift the weight.
13. The tale was about a cat with a long ________________.

Word Story In France long ago, a bag used to carry letters was called a **male**. One spelling word sounds the same but is spelled differently. It means "letters and packages." Write the word.

14. ________________

Family Tree: paint Think about how the **paint** words are alike in spelling and meaning. Then add another **paint** word to the tree.

Name ______________________ Date ____________

Spelling in Context

Use each spelling word once to complete the poem.

The Letter

What would you do if you saw a long tail
Sticking out of a letter you got in the ____________?
1
Would you yell, "This thing belongs in a ____________!"?
2
Would you feed it a worm or maybe a ____________?
3
Would you jump in a boat and put up a ____________?
4
Would you chew a finger and bite a ____________?
5
Would you ____________ a sign that said, "For Sale"?
6
If you called the police because you started to worry,
Do you think ____________ would come in a hurry?
7
Would you take the thing out and twist it
Into the shape of an ____________,
8

Name ______________________ Date ____________

Or would you leave it alone and look at it
And wait and wait and ______________?
9
Would you wrap it in paper that's plain?
Would you send it away on a ______________?
10
Would you leave it outside in the ______________?
11
Would you tie it all up with a ______________?
12
Would you wonder how many pounds it could
______________?
13
I know what I'd do if I saw a long ______________
14
Sticking out of a letter I got in the mail.
I'd open the letter, and then with a shout
I'd say, "Hi there, Lizard! It's time to come out!"

chain
gain
eight
tail
paint
nail
pail
they
snail
rain
wait
mail
train
sail

★ Challenge Yourself ★

Challenge Words

bravery
dainty
faithful

What do you think each Challenge Word means? Check a dictionary to see if you are right. Then use the Challenge Words to write sentences on separate paper.

15. It took **bravery** to jump off the high diving board.

16. The dress was covered with **dainty** flowers.

17. A **faithful** pet will never run away from home.

Name ______________________ Date ____________

Lesson 15: Words with *-ed* or *-ing*

fishing

1. -ed Words

1. ____________
2. ____________
3. ____________
4. ____________
5. ____________
6. ____________
7. ____________

2. -ing Words

1. ____________
2. ____________
3. ____________
4. ____________
5. ____________
6. ____________
7. ____________

helping
tricked
wishing
ended
fishing
wished
dressing
picking
handed
thanked
thinking
asked
fished
catching

Say and Listen

Say the spelling words. Listen for the ending sounds.

Think and Sort

A **base word** is a word that can be used to make other words.

Each spelling word is made of a base word and the ending **-ed** or **-ing**.

Look at each word. Think about the base word and the ending. Spell each word aloud.

1. Write the seven spelling words that end in **-ed**.
2. Write the seven spelling words that end in **-ing**.

Use the steps on page iv to study words that are hard for you.

Spelling Patterns

The endings **-ed** and **-ing** can be added to base words to make new words.

fish + **ed** = fish**ed**	fish + **ing** = fish**ing**

Name ______________________ Date ____________

Spelling and Meaning

Antonyms Antonyms are words that have opposite meanings. Write the spelling word that is an antonym of each word below.

1. answered ____________
2. began ____________
3. hurting ____________
4. throwing ____________

Clues Write the spelling word for each clue.

5. what you did if you caught some fish ____________
6. what you did if you were polite ____________
7. what you did when you hoped ____________
8. sitting with bait at the end of a pole ____________
9. taking an apple from a tree ____________
10. putting clothes on ____________
11. what someone did to play a joke on you ____________
12. what you are doing if you are hoping ____________
13. using your brain ____________

Word Story One spelling word comes from the very old word **capere. Capere** meant "to get hold of." All the letters except the first two have changed. Write the spelling word that means "getting hold of."

14. ____________

Family Tree: thinking Thinking is a form of **think**. Think about how the **think** words are alike in spelling and meaning. Then add another **think** word to the tree.

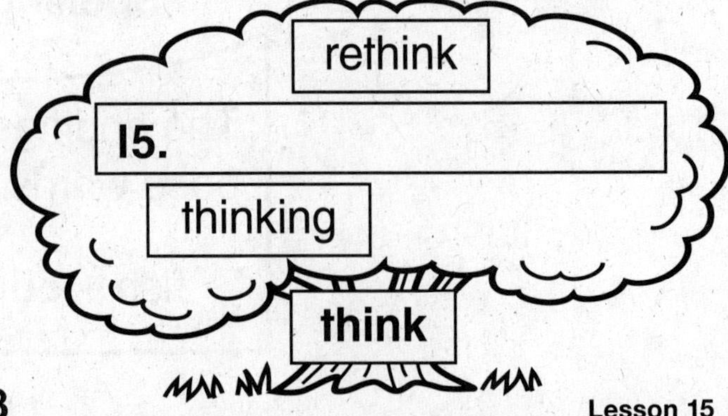

Name ______________________ Date ____________

Spelling in Context

Use each spelling word once to complete the story.

Rabbit and Turtle

Rabbit spent most of his time teasing Turtle. He teased Turtle for walking slowly. Turtle ________ (1) he could run as fast as Rabbit. One day Turtle was ________ (2) he could beat Rabbit in a race. He wrote a note and ________ (3) it to Rabbit.

Meet me under
the oak tree
for a race to
the river. Owl
will be the
judge.

Rabbit got all dressed up for the race. He put on his new purple running shoes and a bright headband. He spent quite a long time ________ (4) himself. Turtle just wore his shell.

The race began at noon. Rabbit dashed past Turtle. Soon he was far ahead. He stopped and began ________ (5) berries. Then he saw a pond and went ________ (6). He sat and ________ (7) for a long time. He did not know that Turtle was slowly ________ (8) up with him.

Soon Turtle passed Rabbit. But Turtle was so quiet that Rabbit never saw him. Turtle kept slowly walking. At last he saw the river and the finish line.

Name ______________________ Date __________

When Turtle crossed the finish line, Owl said that the race had ___9___. She gave Turtle a blue ribbon, and Turtle ___10___ her politely.

A minute later Rabbit came running by, holding the five fish he had caught. He ___11___ Owl for his blue ribbon. Then he saw that Turtle had the ribbon. "How could you win? You must have ___12___ me! Did you have friends ___13___ you?"

"No," said Turtle. "I had my own four feet. And I just kept ___14___ that slow but sure wins the race!"

- helping
- tricked
- wishing
- ended
- fishing
- wished
- dressing
- picking
- handed
- thanked
- thinking
- asked
- fished
- catching

★ Challenge Yourself ★

Challenge Words

denying
claimed
alerting

What do you think each Challenge Word means? Check a dictionary to see if you are right. Then use the Challenge Words to write sentences on separate paper.

15. My friend **claimed** she saw a purple cow.

16. Diego kept **denying** that he had eaten the cookies.

17. The alarm is **alerting** the police.

Name ______________________ Date ______________

Lesson 16: Words with Long *e*

feet

1. **e** Words

____
____
____
____

2. **ee** Words

____
____
____
____
____
____
____
____

3. **e**-consonant-**e** Word

____

4. **eo** Word

____

we
people
see
green
she
he
keep
feet
these
bees
street
week
being
three

Say and Listen

Say each spelling word. Listen for the vowel sound you hear in **we**.

Think and Sort

The vowel sound in **we** is called long **e**. All of the spelling words have the long **e** sound. Spell each word aloud.

1. Write the four words with long **e** spelled **e**.
2. Write the eight words with long **e** spelled **ee**.
3. Write the one word with long **e** spelled **e**-consonant-**e**.
4. Write the one word with long **e** spelled **eo**.

Use the steps on page iv to study words that are hard for you.

Spelling Patterns

The long **e** sound can be spelled **e**, **ee**, **e**-consonant-**e**, or **eo**.

e	**ee**	**e**-consonant-**e**	**eo**
w**e**	k**ee**p	th**e**s**e**	p**eo**ple

Name ______________________ Date ____________

Spelling and Meaning

Word Groups Write the spelling word that belongs in each group.

1. ants, wasps, ____________
2. yellow, ____________, red
3. legs, ____________, toes
4. ____________, him, his
5. day, ____________, month
6. ____________, her, hers
7. them, those, ____________
8. ____________, us, our

Synonyms Synonyms are words that have the same meaning. Write the spelling word that is a synonym for each word below.

9. look ____________
10. persons ____________
11. road ____________
12. acting ____________
13. save ____________

Word Story One of the spelling words is the name for a number. It is written **drei** in German, **trois** in French, and **tres** in Spanish. Long ago the word was spelled **thre**. Write the word.

14. ____________

Family Tree: see Think about how the **see** words are alike in spelling and meaning. Then add another **see** word to the tree.

Name ______________________________ Date ____________

Spelling in Context

Use each spelling word once to complete the story.

Grandfather's Race

Kevin and Abby went to ______________ (1) a bicycle race. The race was more than ______________ (2) miles long. Many ______________ (3) came to watch the race. Police stood near the ______________ (4). Their job was to ______________ (5) people away from the racers.

The bicycles came around the corner. A rider in a bright ______________ (6) shirt was in front. "Hey! That's your grandfather!" yelled Kevin. "I've never seen him go so fast. How does ______________ (7) do it?"

"By pedaling his ______________ (8) really fast!" Abby said. "He's also riding a racing bike. On our bikes, ______________ (9)

Name ________________________ Date ______________

could never go that fast." After the race, Abby ran to her grandfather. "You won!" ____________ (10) shouted happily. Then she saw the ____________ (11).

Her grandfather jumped around and ducked his head. "Ouch!" he yelled. "Well, I wasn't ____________ (12) very careful," he told Abby. "I bumped into a beehive. Out came the bees. I didn't know how fast I could ride until I tried to race ____________ (13) bees. I won't be able to touch my neck for a ____________ (14). Let's get out of here! I beat all the other racers, but I lost the race with the bees!"

- we
- people
- see
- green
- she
- he
- keep
- feet
- these
- bees
- street
- week
- being
- three

★ Challenge Yourself ★

Challenge Words

athlete
freeze
belief

What do you think each Challenge Word means? Check a dictionary to see if you are right. Then use the Challenge Words to write sentences on separate paper.

15. The best **athlete** was given a blue ribbon.

16. The ponds here **freeze** every winter.

17. My **belief** is that stealing is wrong.

Name ______________________ Date ____________

Lesson 17: More Words with Long *e*

puppy

1. ea Words

____

____

____

____

____

____

____

____

2. y Words

____

____

____

____

____

____

happy
clean
very
please
leap
funny
peach
eat
city
heat
puppy
dream
penny
mean

Say and Listen

Say each spelling word. Listen for the long **e** sound.

Think and Sort

All of the spelling words have the long **e** sound. Spell each word aloud.

Look at the letters in each word. Think about how long **e** is spelled. How many spellings for long **e** do you see?

1. Write the eight spelling words that have long **e** spelled **ea**.
2. Write the six spelling words that have long **e** spelled **y**.

Use the steps on page iv to study words that are hard for you.

Spelling Patterns

The long **e** sound can be spelled **ea** or **y**.

ea	**y**
eat	happ**y**

Name ______________________ Date __________

Spelling and Meaning

Antonyms Antonyms are words that have opposite meanings. Write the spelling word that is an antonym of the word in dark type.

1. The clown made us feel ______________. **sad**
2. Please wear a ______________ shirt. **dirty**
3. Do not be ______________ to animals. **kind**
4. You can ______________ this in the oven. **cool**

Clues Write the spelling word for each clue.

5. This place has many people and buildings. ______________
6. Say this to ask for something. ______________
7. This fruit has a fuzzy skin. ______________
8. Frogs do this to move. ______________
9. Use this word instead of **silly**. ______________
10. People do this to food. ______________
11. Every big dog was once this. ______________
12. This coin is worth one cent. ______________
13. When you are asleep, you do this. ______________

Word Story Many English words come from Latin. Latin was the language spoken in Rome long ago. One spelling word comes from the Latin word **verus**. It meant "truly" or "really." Write the spelling word.

14. ______________

Family Tree: clean Think about how the **clean** words are alike in spelling and meaning. Then add another **clean** word to the tree.

cleaning

15.

cleanly

unclean

clean

Name ______________________________ Date ____________

Spelling in Context

Use each spelling word once to complete the story.

Lucky Penny

It was a hot summer day in the ______________(1). A ______________(2) and a dime lay on the sidewalk. They were hoping someone would pick them up. The dime was becoming very grouchy because of the ______________(3). "No one's ever going to pick you up," it said to the penny.

"Don't be so ______________(4) to me," said the penny. "I might make someone ______________(5) someday."

"No one wants a penny these days," snapped the dime. "You can't buy an apple or a ______________(6) with a penny. You can't buy anything to ______________(7) with a penny. You can't buy a pet with a penny, either," the dime went on. "You can't buy a kitten or a ______________(8) or a goldfish."

The dime was making the penny feel sad. "Some days I ______________(9) about being a

Name ______________________ Date ____________

new penny," it said. "I'm dirty and old now. Once I was shiny and ____________."

Just then a girl 10 came by and stopped. The penny got a ____________ feeling. The little girl was squeezing the 11 penny in her hand. "Here's an old one!" she cried. "May I ____________ keep it, Grandma?"

Her grandmother said, 12 "This is a ____________ old penny, Rosa. It would be a very good one 13 to collect."

The penny felt its heart ____________ for joy. Rosa put the penny in her pocket 14 and gave the dime to her grandmother.

"Good-bye, dime," the penny sang out. "Do you see? I do make someone happy!"

happy
clean
very
please
leap
funny
peach
eat
city
heat
puppy
dream
penny
mean

★ Challenge Yourself ★

Challenge Words

disease
cheap
cheat

Use a dictionary to answer these questions. Then use the Challenge Words to write sentences on separate paper.

15. Can a net catch a **disease**? ____________

16. Is a meal **cheap** if it costs fifty cents? ____________

17. Can a person **cheat** on a lamp? ____________

Name ______________________ Date __________

Lesson 18: Words with Long *i*

bike

1. i-consonant-e Words

____
____
____
____
____
____
____
____
____
____
____
____

2. i Word

____

3. eye Word

____

like
find
ice
bike
side
nine
write
mine
ride
white
eye
hide
inside
five

Say and Listen

Say each spelling word. Listen for the vowel sound you hear in **like**.

Think and Sort

The vowel sound in **like** is called long **i**. All of the spelling words have the long **i** sound. Spell each word aloud.

Look at the letters in each word. Think about how long **i** is spelled.

1. Write the twelve words with long **i** spelled **i**-consonant-**e**.
2. Write the one word with long **i** spelled **i**.
3. Write the one word with long **i** spelled **eye**.

Use the steps on page iv to study words that are hard for you.

Spelling Patterns

The long **i** sound can be spelled **i**-consonant-**e**, **i**, or **eye**.

i-consonant-**e**	**i**	**eye**
ride	find	eye

Name ______________________________ Date ____________

Spelling and Meaning

Word Meanings Write the spelling word for each meaning. Use a dictionary if you need to.

1. something with wheels to ride on ________________
2. to enjoy ________________
3. to sit on and be carried ________________
4. the lightest color ________________
5. to make words with a pencil ________________
6. into ________________

Rhymes Write the spelling word that completes each sentence and rhymes with the underlined word.

7. Let's ________________ out how to wind the clock.
8. Did you try to blink your left ________________?
9. Did the cat ________________ under the slide?
10. We planted all ________________ of the pine trees.
11. The left ________________ of the road is wide.
12. I slipped twice on the snow and ________________.
13. Her soup is cold, but ________________ is fine.

Word Story Long ago English people used the word **fimfi** to name the number after four. The word later became **fif**. Write the spelling we use now.

14. ________________

Family Tree: white Think about how the **white** words are alike in spelling and meaning. Then add another **white** word to the tree.

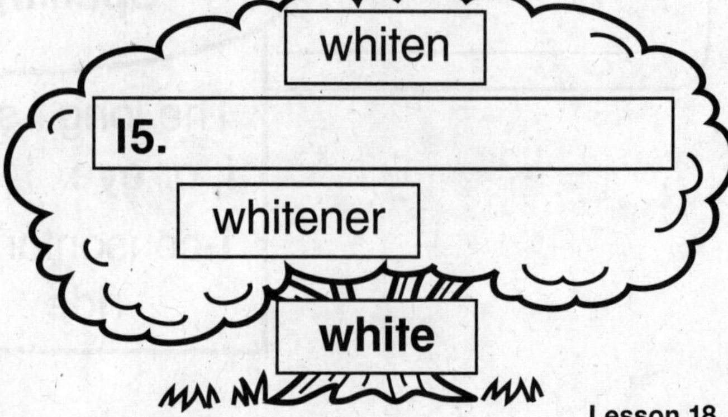

Name ______________________________ Date ____________

Spelling in Context

Use each spelling word once to complete the story.

Arctic Explorer

December 8

Dear Diary,

Today I want to ______________ (1) about the Arctic. An uncle of ______________ (2) lived in the Arctic from 1990 to 1999. That's ______________ (3) whole years! He said there was snow as far as the ______________ (4) could see.

I would ______________ (5) to explore the Arctic. All that snow and ______________ (6) would be beautiful to see. I could ______________ (7) a dog sled across it. That would be more fun than riding my ______________ (8)!

I would look for animals that ______________ (9) from other animals in the snow.

I would build a snow house and live in it, too. I could

Name ______________________ Date ____________

look out and see miles of ____________ snow. If I found a little animal that was hurt, I could bring it ____________ the house. I would take care of it.
(10, 11)

It would be fun to spend ____________ or six years going all over the Arctic. I would ride from one ____________ to the other. Maybe I would ____________ one little place that no one else has discovered. Then I would be famous.
(12, 13, 14)

My uncle said that he will take me to the Arctic if he ever goes again. We could explore it together. I hope he decides to go soon!

like
find
ice
bike
side
nine
write
mine
ride
white
eye
hide
inside
five

★ Challenge Yourself ★

Challenge Words

license
climate
advice

Write the Challenge Word for each clue. Check a dictionary to see if you are right. Then use the Challenge Words to write sentences on separate paper.

15. You might give this to a friend. ____________

16. You need one to drive a car. ____________

17. The North Pole has a cold one. The desert has a hot one. ____________

Name ______________________ Date ______________

Lesson 19: More Words with Long *i*

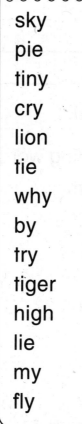

tiger

1. i Words

____

____

____

2. y Words

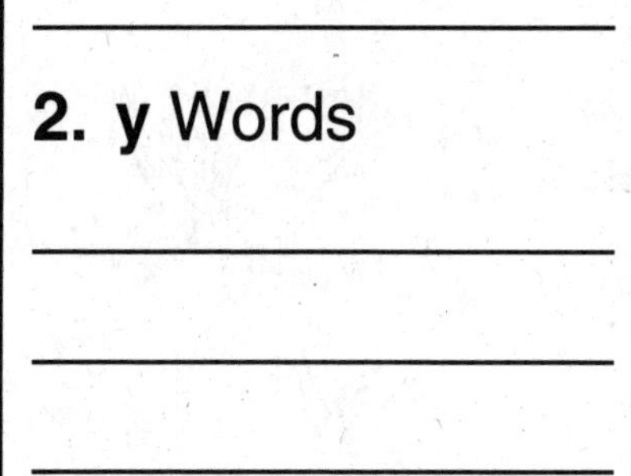

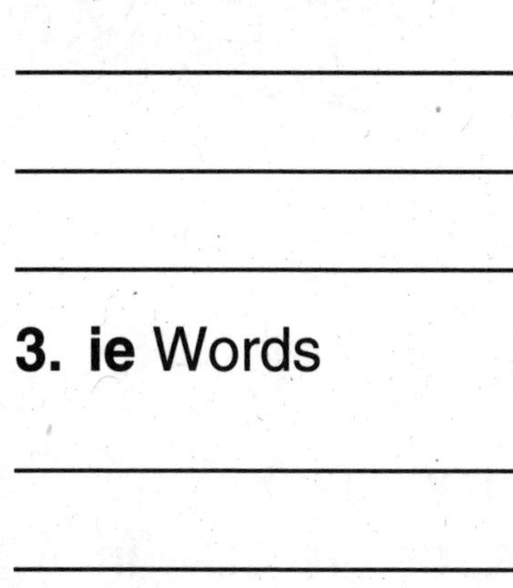

3. ie Words

____

____

____

4. igh Word

____

sky
pie
tiny
cry
lion
tie
why
by
try
tiger
high
lie
my
fly

Say and Listen

Say each spelling word.
Listen for the long **i** sound.

Think and Sort

All of the spelling words have the long **i** sound. Spell each word aloud.

Look at the letters in each word. Think about how long **i** is spelled.

1. Write the three spelling words with long **i** spelled **i**.
2. Write the seven spelling words with long **i** spelled **y**.
3. Write the three spelling words with long **i** spelled **ie**.
4. Write the one spelling word with long **i** spelled **igh**.

Use the steps on page iv to study words that are hard for you.

Spelling Patterns

The long **i** sound can be spelled **i**, **y**, **ie**, or **igh**.

i	y	ie	igh
tiny	sky	pie	high

Name ______________________________ Date ______________

Spelling and Meaning

Antonyms Antonyms are words that have opposite meanings. Write the spelling word that is an antonym of each underlined word.

1. The cat climbed to the <u>low</u> branch. ______________
2. Don't <u>laugh</u> over spilled milk. ______________
3. Look at that <u>large</u> mouse! ______________
4. He was sorry he told the <u>truth</u>. ______________
5. This is <u>your</u> hat. ______________

What's Missing? Write the missing spelling words.

6. eat ______________ and ice cream
7. wear a shirt and ______________
8. the mane on the ______________
9. ______________ and try again
10. don't know ______________
11. clouds in the ______________
12. stripes on the ______________
13. sit ______________ him

Word Story How would you like to **fliugan**? That's an Old German word. In Old English it was **fleogan**. The word tells what birds and airplanes do. Write the spelling word as it is spelled today.

14. ______________

Family Tree: try Think about how the **try** words are alike in spelling and meaning. Then add another **try** word to the tree.

Name ______________________________ Date ____________

Spelling in Context

Use each spelling word once to complete the story.

Cloud Watching

On windy spring days, I like to ________________ (1) on my back and watch the clouds in the ________________ (2). Clouds used to look like big white puffs to me. I ________________ (3) to look at them carefully now. I see some real surprises!

The sky today has lots of clouds. One of them has stripes like a ________________ (4). I watch a bird ________________ (5) past it. Watch out, bird! Above me is a horse with a long tail. The tail begins to curl. I watch it ________________ (6) itself into a knot.

A cloud way up ________________ (7) is a very tasty surprise. It's an apple ________________ (8).

Name ______________________________ Date ____________

It looks like it is missing a ______________ little bite.
                                              9
Maybe that mouse cloud sailed ______________ it
                                                10
and nibbled on it.

Above the school are two ______________ cubs.
                                            11
Their mouths are open. I think they are starting to

______________ for the mother lion. I never feel
      12
like crying while I'm watching clouds. I could spend

______________ whole day looking at them. Do you
      13
see ______________ it is so much fun?
          14

sky
pie
tiny
cry
lion
tie
why
by
try
tiger
high
lie
my
fly

★ Challenge Yourself ★

Challenge Words
tying
rhyme
diet

What do you think each Challenge Word means? Check a dictionary to see if you are right. Then use the Challenge Words to write sentences on separate paper.

15. Amy is **tying** her shoelaces.

16. I like to write poems that **rhyme**.

17. Some animals can live on a **diet** of fish.

Name ______________________ Date ______________

Lesson 20: More Words with *-ed* or *-ing*

running

1. -ed Words

____
____
____
____
____
____
____

2. -ing Words

____
____
____
____
____
____
____

dropping
cutting
dropped
spotted
stopping
hopped
jogged
jogging
running
shopped
hopping
stopped
dotted
shopping

Say and Listen

Say the spelling words. Listen for the ending sounds.

Think and Sort

Each spelling word is made by adding **-ed** or **-ing** to a base word. Each base word ends with a short vowel and consonant.

Look at the letters in each spelling word. Think about how the base word changes when **-ed** or **-ing** is added. Spell each word aloud.

1. Write the seven spelling words that end in **-ed**.
2. Write the seven spelling words that end in **-ing**.

Use the steps on page iv to study words that are hard for you.

Spelling Patterns

Some base words end with a short vowel and a consonant. The final consonant is usually doubled when **-ed** or **-ing** is added.

hop + **ed** = hop**ped** | hop + **ing** = hop**ping**

Name ______________________________ Date ____________

Spelling and Meaning

Word Meanings Write the spelling word for each meaning.

1. moved up and down quickly ________________
2. moving at a slow, steady trot ________________
3. marked with a round point ________________
4. ended ________________
5. looked for things to buy ________________
6. let something fall ________________

Synonyms Synonyms are words that have the same meaning. Write the spelling word that is a synonym for each word in dark type.

7. The apples are ________________ off the tree. **falling**
8. The woman ________________ around the block. **trotted**
9. We saw that the rain was ________________. **ending**
10. The children are ________________ on one foot. **jumping**
11. We saw a man ________________ to his car. **racing**
12. The spilled paint ________________ the floor. **marked**
13. Mom is ________________ for some new shoes. **looking**

Word Story In Iceland long ago, **kuti** meant "knife." In Old English the word became **cutten** and meant "to cut." One of the spelling words comes from **kuti** and **cutten**. Write the word.

14. ________________

Family Tree: spotted **Spotted** is a form of **spot**. Think about how the **spot** words are alike in spelling and meaning. Then add another **spot** word to the tree.

Name ______________________________ Date ____________

Spelling in Context

Use each spelling word once to complete the poem.

Stop Benny's Hops!

Benny was hopping and ________________.
1
He hopped and hopped without ________________!
2
His friends liked his trick
And watched him hop on his stick
For an hour and a half without ________________.
3
Benny said running was not fun.
"If you run, you're just like everyone.
When I'm hopping, I'm soaring!
I think ________________ is boring,"
4
Said Benny while eating a bun.
His family went ________________ with Benny.
5
His mother said, "Benny looks silly.
He has hopped and ________________
6
Every time that we've ________________.
7
He will never stop, will he?"
Benny knocked over plants that were potted
And the living room rug became ________________.
8
"Benny, hop outdoors,

Name ______________________________ Date ______________

Not on these floors.

With mud our rug is all ________________!"
9

Benny's father didn't know what to do

With a son like a strange kangaroo.

"It's time that he ________________!
10

I want that pogo stick ________________,
11

Or else he'll soon live at the zoo!"

Benny's pogo stick rests on the floor.

"I'm afraid I can't hop anymore.

I'm ________________ the hopping short,
12

I'll go ________________ for sport."
13

And he happily ________________ out the door.
14

- dropping
- cutting
- dropped
- spotted
- stopping
- hopped
- jogged
- jogging
- running
- shopped
- hopping
- stopped
- dotted
- shopping

★ Challenge Yourself ★

Challenge Words

admitting
strutting
propped

What do you think each Challenge Word means? Check a dictionary to see if you are right. Then use the Challenge Words to write sentences on separate paper.

15. **Admitting** a mistake is hard.

16. The rooster was **strutting** around the barnyard.

17. I **propped** my bat against the fence.

Name ______________________ Date ____________

Lesson 21: Words with Long *o*

nose

1. o Words

____
____
____

2. o-consonant-e Words

____
____
____
____
____
____
____

3. ow Words

____
____
____
____

go
yellow
home
rope
grow
know
no
nose
hope
stone
snow
so
hole
joke

Say and Listen

Say each spelling word. Listen for the vowel sound you hear in **go**.

Think and Sort

The vowel sound in all of the spelling words is called long **o**. Spell each word aloud.

Look at the letters in each word. Think about how long **o** is spelled.

1. Write the three spelling words with long **o** spelled **o**.
2. Write the seven spelling words with long **o** spelled **o**-consonant-**e**.
3. Write the four spelling words with long **o** spelled **ow**.

Use the steps on page iv to study words that are hard for you.

Spelling Patterns

The long **o** sound can be spelled **o**, **o**-consonant-**e**, or **ow**.

o	o-consonant-e	ow
go	hole	snow

Name ______________________ Date ____________

Spelling and Meaning

Word Groups Write the spelling word that belongs in each group.

1. rain, ______________, ice
2. red, blue, ______________
3. eye, ear, ______________
4. yes, ______________, maybe
5. string, yarn, ______________

Rhymes Write the spelling word that completes each sentence and rhymes with the underlined word.

6. I left my brush and comb at ______________.
7. The tiny mole ran down a ______________.
8. I ______________ you like the fancy soap.
9. The dinosaur bone turned to ______________.
10. Ned woke me up to tell me a ______________.
11. Corn plants will ______________ in each row.
12. The bow was ______________ big that it hid the package.
13. I cannot ______________ skating with a sore toe.

Word Story One spelling word was once spelled **cnowen**. The word meant "to recognize." Today the word begins with a silent letter. Write the word.

14. ______________

Family Tree: hope Think about how the **hope** words are alike in spelling and meaning. Then add another **hope** word to the tree.

Name ______________________________ Date ______________

Spelling in Context

Use each spelling word once to complete the story.

Jump Rope Rose

Rose's leg was in a cast. It all started when she went ________________ (1) skiing. She put on her new ski hat. When she started to ________________ (2) down a tall hill, the ski hat slid down to her ________________ (3) and covered her eyes. She couldn't see the deep ________________ (4) in the trail. Rose fell and hit her leg on a large ________________ (5). The leg was broken.

At first having a cast was fun for Rose. Her friends wrote on it. They visited her at ________________ (6) and told her funny stories. Her father brought her a pot of bulbs, and she watched them ________________ (7) into pink tulips. But then spring came, and everyone but Rose was playing outside and jumping ________________ (8). There was ________________ (9) way Rose could jump rope with a cast on.

"I ________________ (10) the doctor will take my cast off today," Rose said to her mother. "I want to jump rope with my friends."

Name ______________________ Date ____________

"Maybe he will," her mother replied, "but we really don't ______________ for sure."
11

They went to the doctor's office. Rose stared at Dr. Bradford. He had a big cast on his foot!

"Hello, Rose," he said. "Look what I did water skiing. You are lucky. Today your cast comes off, but mine just went on!"

Rose felt sorry for Dr. Bradford. She told him a funny ______________. The next day she sent him a
12
big pot of ______________ tulips. She knew how Dr.
13
Bradford felt. She was ______________ happy that
14
her cast was off!

- go
- yellow
- home
- rope
- grow
- know
- no
- nose
- hope
- stone
- snow
- so
- hole
- joke

★ Challenge Yourself ★

Challenge Words

hopeful
explode
bony

Write the Challenge Word for each clue. Check a dictionary to see if you are right. Then use the Challenge Words to write sentences on separate paper.

15. A very thin horse is this. ______________

16. You are this when you want a good thing to happen. ______________

17. Firecrackers do this on the Fourth of July. ______________

Name ______________________ Date ______________

Lesson 22: More Words with Long *o*

goat

1. o Words

____
____
____
____
____
____
____
____
____
____

2. oa Words

____
____
____
____

cold
road
gold
goat
old
coat
sold
boat
open
over
roll
most
hold
told

Say and Listen

Say each spelling word. Listen for the long **o** sound.

Think and Sort

All of the spelling words have the long **o** sound. Spell each word aloud.

Look at the letters in each word. Think about how long **o** is spelled. How many spellings for long **o** do you see?

1. Write the ten spelling words that have long **o** spelled **o**.
2. Write the four spelling words that have long **o** spelled **oa**.

Use the steps on page iv to study words that are hard for you.

Spelling Patterns

The long **o** sound can be spelled **o** or **oa**.

o	**oa**
cold	goat

Name ______________________ Date ____________

Spelling and Meaning

Letter Scramble Unscramble the letters in dark type to make a spelling word. Write the word on the line.

1. **atoc** ______________ and hat
2. **roev** under or ______________
3. **dols** bought and ______________
4. **locd** hot and ______________
5. **enpo** ______________ or closed

Clues Write the spelling word for each clue.

6. This travels on the water. ______________
7. This word means "did tell." ______________
8. Many rings are made of this. ______________
9. A car drives on this. ______________
10. This farm animal has horns. ______________
11. You can do this to someone's hand. ______________
12. The opposite of **new** is this. ______________
13. This word rhymes with **toast**. ______________

Word Story Long ago the word **rotula** meant "small wheel." Later the word became **rollen** and meant "to turn over and over." What word do we use today? Write the spelling word.

14. ______________

Family Tree: open Think about how the **open** words are alike in spelling and meaning. Then add another **open** word to the tree.

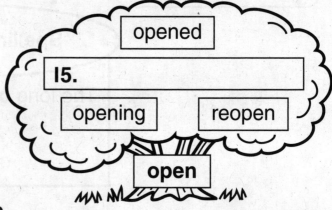

opened

15. ______________

opening

reopen

open

Name ______________________________ Date ____________

Spelling in Context

Use each spelling word once to complete the story.

The Goat Boat

It was winter. Peter and his family were hungry and ________________.
1
They lived in a small ________________
2
house far out in the country. To make

money, the family ________________ goat's milk to people passing
3
by. But this winter the narrow dirt ________________ past their
4
farm was closed. The snow was much too deep. One day Peter watched his mother ________________ their last bag of beans.
5
They would soon be out of food! Peter had to find a job in the city. Nothing was going to ________________ him back.
6

Peter called his two goats. He took the oars out of his fishing ________________. He tied each ________________ to the boat.
7 8
He put on his ________________ and packed a ________________
9 10
to eat on the way to the city. Then Peter ________________ his
11
family good-bye.

Name ______________________ Date __________

Peter and his goats had fun as they slid

______ (12) the hills. People came running and asking for rides. Peter got an idea.

"Yes, you may have a ride!" he told them. "But you must pay me because I must have money to buy food."

The people were happy to pay Peter for a ride in his snow boat. It was the ______ (13) fun they had ever had!

Peter never got to the city. At the end of the day, he went home to his family with a pocket full of ______ (14) coins. Every winter day he took people for rides. He and his family never had to worry about being hungry again.

cold
road
gold
goat
old
coat
sold
boat
open
over
roll
most
hold
told

★ Challenge Yourself ★

Challenge Words

mold
boulder
clover

Use a dictionary to answer each question. Then use the Challenge Words to write sentences on separate paper.

15. Can you put water in a **mold** to make ice cubes? ______

16. Can you pick up a **boulder** with just one hand? ______

17. Would you look for a four-leaf **clover** in a field? ______

Name ______________________ Date ______________

Lesson 23: The Vowel Sound in *book*

book

1. oo Words

____

____

____

____

____

____

____

____

2. ou Words

____

____

____

3. u Words

____

____

____

book
put
look
could
pull
would
cook
should
full
stood
cookies
good
foot
took

Say and Listen

Say each spelling word. Listen for the vowel sound you hear in **book**.

Think and Sort

All of the spelling words have the vowel sound in **book**. Spell each word aloud.

Look at the letters in each word. Think about how the vowel sound in **book** is spelled.

1. Write the eight spelling words that have **oo**.
2. Write the three spelling words that have **ou**.
3. Write the three spelling words that have **u**.

Use the steps on page iv to study words that are hard for you.

Spelling Patterns

The vowel sound in **book** can be spelled **oo**, **ou**, or **u**.

oo	ou	u
book	could	put

Name ______________________________ Date ____________

Spelling and Meaning

Word Meanings Write the spelling word for each meaning.

1. someone who makes food ________________
2. a form of the word **will** ________________
3. small, sweet cakes ________________
4. to set something in place ________________
5. pages fastened together ________________
6. was able to do something ________________
7. was upright on the feet ________________
8. to have a duty ________________
9. see ________________

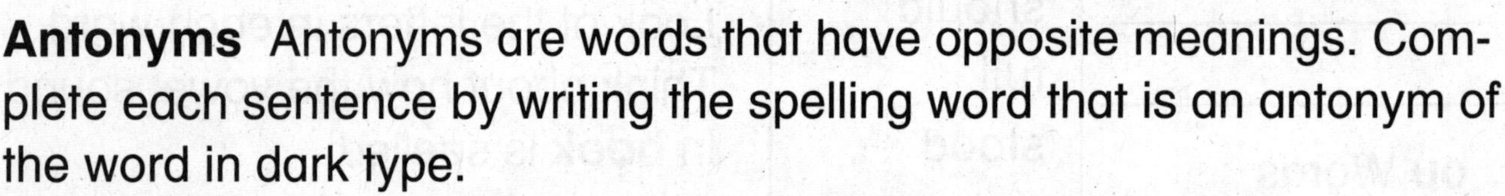

Antonyms Antonyms are words that have opposite meanings. Complete each sentence by writing the spelling word that is an antonym of the word in dark type.

10. Rita will ________________ your sled up the hill. **push**
11. Mason ________________ a cookie to school. **gave**
12. The cookie jar was ________________. **empty**
13. This spaghetti tastes ________________. **bad**

Word Story One spelling word was once spelled **fot**. It named the part of the leg you stand on. The meaning has not changed, but the spelling has. Write the spelling we use today.

14. ________________

Family Tree: cook Think about how the **cook** words are alike in spelling and meaning. Then add another **cook** word to the tree.

Name ______________________________ Date ____________

Spelling in Context

Use each spelling word once to complete the story.

The Fable of the Cookie

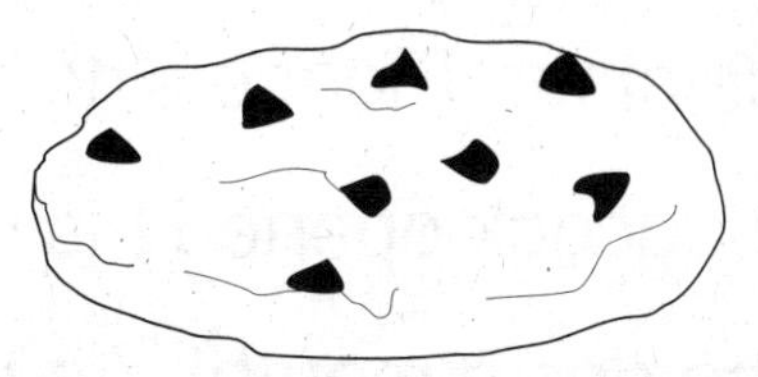

One day a man bought some chocolate chip ______________ (1). He carried them home in a bag. The bag broke, and two cookies fell out.

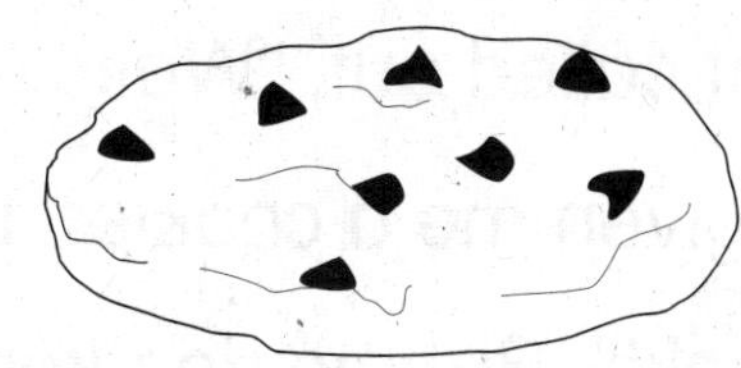

A peacock found the cookies on the grass. "These cookies smell so ______________ (2)! They must have been baked by a fine ______________ (3)!" said the peacock. He ______________ (4) the cookies and hopped into a tree.

A dog was passing by. She smelled the chocolate chip cookies. She ______________ (5) below the tree and said, "Please, dear Peacock, ______________ (6) me up into the tree. I will help you eat your cookies."

The peacock ______________ (7) not help the dog. The hungry dog began to stamp her ______________ (8).

A wise old cat walked by. "Dear Cat, ______________ (9) you help me get the cookies?" asked the dog.

"Dear Peacock," purred the cat, "please ______________ (10) the cookies down and fly away so I can ______________ (11) at

Name ______________________ Date ____________

your beautiful feathers." But the peacock would not fly.

The cat said, "I read in a ______________ that
12
peacocks are very good singers, but I have never heard a peacock sing. Please sing for me."

The peacock opened his mouth to sing. The cookies fell into the dog's mouth! As the happy dog ran away, the cat called out, "Wait! You ______________
13
have given me a cookie. I helped you by tricking the peacock!" But the dog kept running.

"We will not have ______________ stomachs
14
today," said the cat and the peacock sadly.

- book
- put
- look
- could
- pull
- would
- cook
- should
- full
- stood
- cookies
- good
- foot
- took

★ Challenge Yourself ★

Challenge Words

bulletin
bushel
cookbook

What do you think each Challenge Word means? Check a dictionary to see if you are right. Then use the Challenge Words to write sentences on separate paper.

15. The **bulletin** on the radio told about a bad storm.

16. A **bushel** of apples will be enough for everyone.

17. Use a **cookbook** to find out how to make bread.

Name ______________________ Date ______________

Lesson 24: The Vowel Sound in *zoo*

food

1. oo Words

____
____
____
____
____
____
____
____

2. ue Word

____

3. ew Word

____

4. o Words

____
____
____
____

zoo
too
to
do
new
room
food
who
blue
school
tooth
soon
moon
two

Say and Listen

Say each spelling word. Listen for the vowel sound you hear in **zoo**.

Think and Sort

All of the spelling words have the vowel sound in **zoo**. Spell each word aloud.

Look at the letters in each spelling word. Think about how the vowel sound in **zoo** is spelled.

1. Write the eight words with **oo**.
2. Write the one word with **ue**.
3. Write the one word with **ew**.
4. Write the four words with **o**.

Use the steps on page iv to study words that are hard for you.

Spelling Patterns

The vowel sound in **zoo** can be spelled **oo**, **ue**, **ew**, or **o**.

oo	ue	ew	o
zoo	blue	new	do

Name ______________________ Date __________

Spelling and Meaning

Word Meanings Write the spelling word for each meaning.

1. a body that moves around a planet __________
2. which person __________
3. a place where wild animals are kept __________
4. something to eat __________
5. in a short time __________
6. a hard, bony growth in the mouth __________
7. a space in a building __________

Homophones Homophones are words that sound the same but have different spellings and meanings. Write the spelling word that completes each sentence and is a homophone of the underlined word.

8. Our __________ umbrella <u>blew</u> away.
9. The <u>two</u> boys swam __________ the shore.
10. I <u>knew</u> that Nina had a __________ puppy.
11. How many books __________ we have <u>due</u> at the library?
12. They have __________ many things <u>to</u> do.
13. Did Chad score __________ points, <u>too</u>?

Word Story Long ago the Greeks spent free time learning things. One meaning of their word **schole** was "free time." One of the spelling words comes from **schole.** Write the word.

14. __________

Family Tree: new Think about how the **new** words are alike in spelling and meaning. Then add another **new** word to the tree.

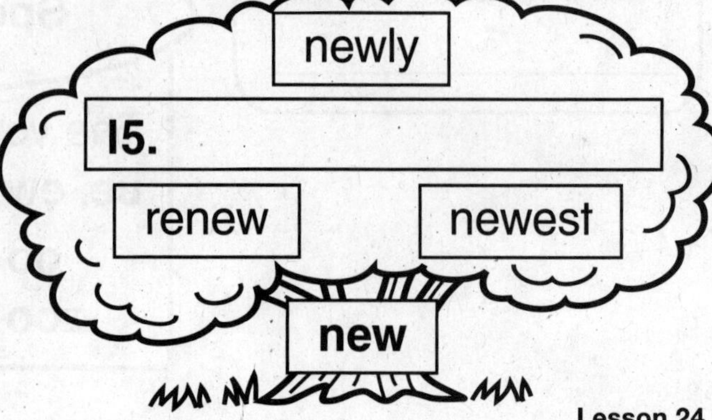

Name ______________________ Date ____________

Spelling in Context

Use each spelling word once to complete the story.

A Fish Story

Many years ago, a big fish lived in the sea. It was as big as a grown-up person. It was ____________ in color.
1

This big fish had six fins on its body. It used its fins ____________ swim quickly. It also had many teeth. Each ____________ was very sharp. The fish used its teeth to catch its ____________ and eat it. Most fish have one tail, but this fish had ____________ tails.
2 3 4 5

Scientists named the fish coelacanth (SEE luh kanth). They thought it had disappeared forever, but they were wrong!

In 1938 some men ____________ were fishing caught a coelacanth. They had never seen such a strange fish. It was so big, there was hardly enough ____________ for it in the net. The men did not know what they had found.
6 7

The men went to a ____________ and asked a teacher what the fish was. The teacher told them they had caught a coelacanth.
8

Name ______________________ Date ____________

The men had not found a ______________ kind of
9
fish. They had found a very old one.

People ______________ began looking for more
10
fish like this one. But it took 14 more years to catch one. One night, by the light of a full ______________,
11
another one was caught. Scientists all over the world were happy to study this fish. They all said it was ______________ good to be true.
12

No ______________ in the world has a coelacanth.
13
But maybe someday you can find one in the ocean. If you ______________, you could become famous!
14

- zoo
- too
- to
- do
- new
- room
- food
- who
- blue
- school
- tooth
- soon
- moon
- two

★ Challenge Yourself ★

Challenge Words

cocoon
bamboo
booth

Write the Challenge Word for each clue. Check a dictionary to see if you are right. Then use the Challenge Words to write sentences on separate paper.

15. This plant makes a good fishing pole. ______________

16. This is what a moth grows in. ______________

17. You can sell lemonade at one of these. ______________

Name ______________________ Date ____________

Lesson 25: More Words with *-ed* or *-ing*

baking

1. -ed Words

____

____

____

____

____

____

____

2. -ing Words

____

____

____

____

____

____

____

joking
named
baking
biked
hoped
living
liked
giving
lived
baked
riding
writing
loved
having

Say and Listen

Say the spelling words. Listen for the ending sounds.

Think and Sort

Each spelling word is made by adding **-ed** or **-ing** to a base word. Each base word ends with **e**.

Look at the letters in each word. Think how the base word changes when **-ed** or **-ing** is added. Spell each word aloud.

1. Write the seven spelling words that end in **-ed**.
2. Write the seven spelling words that end in **-ing**.

Use the steps on page iv to study words that are hard for you.

Spelling Patterns

Some base words end in silent **e**. The **e** is usually dropped before **-ed** or **-ing** is added to these words.

ed	ing
like + ed = **lik**ed	**joke** + ing = **jok**ing

Name ______________________ Date ____________

Spelling and Meaning

Word Groups Write the spelling word that belongs in each group.

1. hiked, skated, ____________
2. reading, spelling, ____________
3. frying, broiling, ____________
4. laughing, teasing, ____________
5. wanted, wished, ____________
6. liked, cared, ____________

Synonyms Synonyms are words that have the same meaning. Complete each sentence by writing the spelling word that is a synonym for each word in dark type.

7. We ____________ the dog Nicki. **called**
8. We ____________ a dozen cookies. **cooked**
9. Mr. Reyna ____________ in a house nearby. **stayed**
10. We are ____________ food to the birds. **offering**
11. Are you ____________ ice cream with your cake? **getting**
12. I like ____________ in the city. **being**
13. Rico will be ____________ on a train. **sitting**

Word Story Long ago in England, **lician** meant "to please." Over time the spelling changed. The meaning became "to enjoy." Write the spelling word that comes from **lician** and means "enjoyed."

14. ____________

Family Tree: liked Think about how the **like** words are alike in spelling and meaning. Then add another **liked** word to the tree.

Name ______________________________ Date ______________

Spelling in Context

Use each spelling word once to complete the story.

Mr. Banana's Invention

Do you know who invented the bicycle and the airplane? A man ________________ Ralph Banana
1
says he did. I talked with Mr. Banana for our school paper. I ________________ to learn the facts.
2

Me: Have you ________________ in many different
3
places?

Mr. B: I've lived in seven countries, if you count the North Pole. I ________________ living there. Are you ________________
4 5
fun talking to me?

Me: Yes, but I'm supposed to ask the questions. How long have you been ________________ in Canada?
6

Mr. B: I moved here right after I invented the airplane.

Me: You must be ________________! Most people say that the
7
Wright brothers invented the airplane.

Mr. B: They did, but I invented the good parts. Be sure you are ________________ all of this down.
8

Name ______________________ Date ____________

I used to be head baker at the North Pole. One day my oven blew up. When the smoke cleared, I saw something interesting.

It was as hard as metal! "My wonderful oven has ______________ something I can ride," I said to myself. I added two wheels and called it a bicycle. I ______________ everywhere. I find that riding a bicycle is much better exercise than ______________ in a car. Don't you? Soon I was ______________ lots of bikes and ______________ them away to everyone at the North Pole. Everyone there ______________ my bicycles!

9 10 11 12 13 14

The next time my oven blew up, I invented the airplane. And this is a true story.

- joking
- named
- baking
- biked
- hoped
- living
- liked
- giving
- lived
- baked
- riding
- writing
- loved
- having

★ Challenge Yourself ★

What do you think each Challenge Word means? Check a dictionary to see if you are right. Then use the Challenge Words to write sentences on separate paper.

Challenge Words

amusing
disliked
lining

15. The clowns were **amusing** the children with funny tricks.

16. Our new kittens **disliked** getting a bath.

17. The fuzzy **lining** in my coat keeps me warm.

Name ____________________ Date ____________

Lesson 26: The Vowel Sound in *out*

cow

1. ou Words

______
______
______
______
______
______
______

2. ow Words

______
______
______
______
______
______
______

out
found
town
sound
now
mouse
flower
round
owl
around
how
house
cow
clown

Say and Listen

Say each spelling word. Listen for the vowel sound you hear in **out.**

Think and Sort

All of the spelling words have the vowel sound in **out**. Spell each word aloud.

Look at the letters in each word. Think about how the vowel sound in **out** is spelled.

1. Write the seven spelling words that have **ou**.
2. Write the seven spelling words that have **ow**.

Use the steps on page iv to study words that are hard for you.

Spelling Patterns

The vowel sound in **out** can be spelled **ou** or **ow**.

ou	**ow**
out	**cow**

Name ______________________ Date ____________

Spelling and Meaning

Letter Scramble Unscramble each group of letters to make a spelling word. Write the word on the line.

1. lerfow ____________
2. undor ____________
3. droanu ____________
4. tou ____________
5. nudof ____________

Clues Write the spelling word for each clue.

6. You see this person at the circus. ____________
7. This is another word for **noise**. ____________
8. This has a roof and a door. ____________
9. Use this word to ask a question. ____________
10. This bird is often called wise. ____________
11. This is a small city. ____________
12. A cat likes to chase this animal. ____________
13. This word is the opposite of **then**. ____________

Word Story In Old English one spelling word was written **cu**. In other languages it was spelled **ku**, **ko**, **cae**, and **bo**. The word names an animal that moos. Write the word.

14. ____________

Family Tree: round Think about how the **round** words are alike in spelling and meaning. Then add another **round** word to the tree.

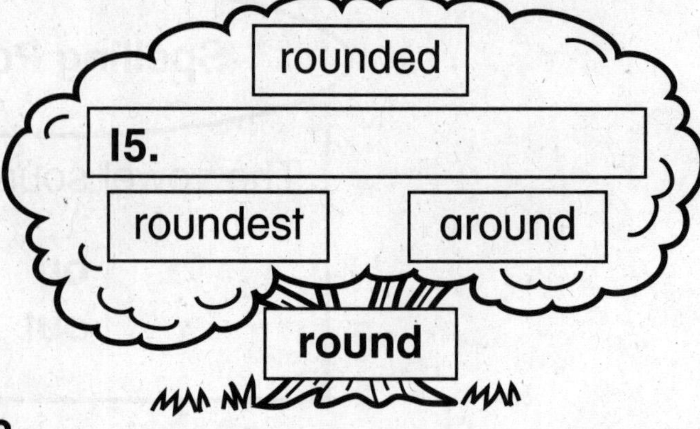

Name ______________________________ Date ____________

Spelling in Context

Use each spelling word once to complete the story.

Drawing by Ana

My name is Ana. My favorite thing to do is draw pictures. People like my pictures because they are funny. I have become a good artist.

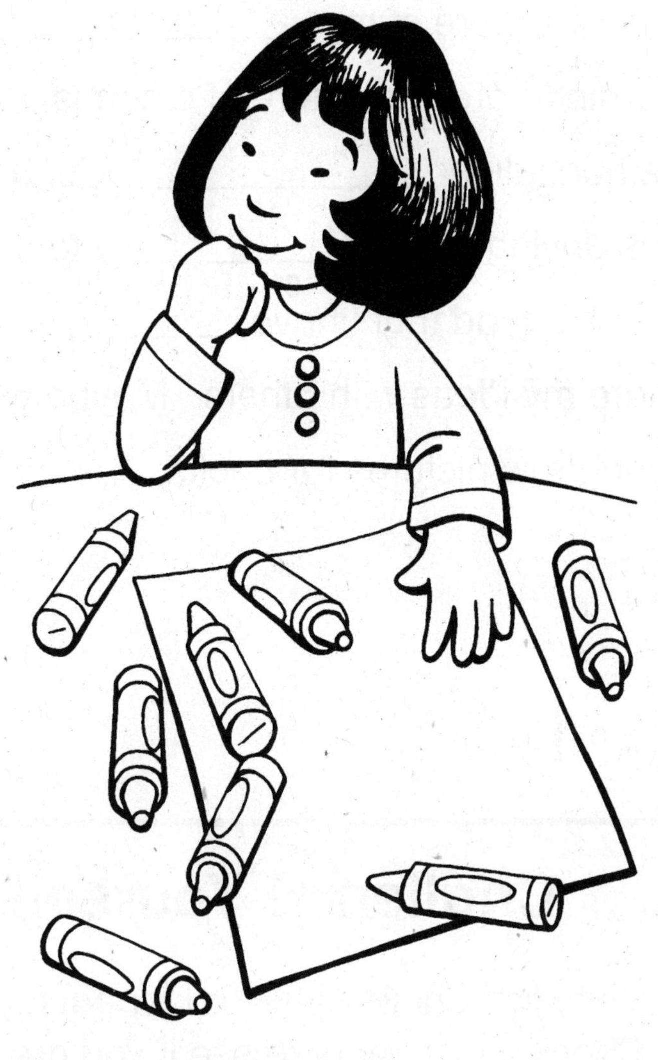

I like to draw animals best. For me it is easy to draw a ________________. I draw
1

________________ circles to
2

make most of the mouse. I draw lines for the whiskers and tail. Right ________________
3

I am drawing a picture of a barnyard. A ________________ is eating hay. A ________________ is
4 5

growing in the ground beside the cow. I will also draw an ________________ in a tree by the barn. I cannot hear, so I have
6

only read about the ________________ that an owl makes at night.
7

Name ______________________ Date __________

Does it really say "Whooo"?

I like drawing animals, but I know ________ (8) to draw lots of other things, too. Yesterday I drew a picture of the stores in my ________ (9). I also drew a picture of my ________ (10) and yard. This morning I drew a picture of a circus ________ (11). He had fallen ________ (12) of a clown car that was driving ________ (13) a tent.

I am glad that I have ________ (14) a way to share my ideas with others. Maybe when I grow up, I can draw pictures for books.

- out
- found
- town
- sound
- now
- mouse
- flower
- round
- owl
- around
- how
- house
- cow
- clown

★ Challenge Yourself ★

Challenge Words

coward
drought
brow

Write the Challenge Word for each clue. Check a dictionary to see if you are right. Then use the Challenge Words to write sentences on separate paper.

15. It is found above your eyes. ________

16. This is a person who is not brave. ________

17. A farmer does not like this. ________

Name ______________________ Date ____________

Lesson 27: The Vowel Sound in *saw*

frog

1. aw Words

____

____

2. a Words

____

____

____

____

____

____

3. o Words

____

____

____

____

____

____

saw
song
talk
dog
call
frog
off
ball
draw
all
lost
small
walk
long

Say and Listen

Say each spelling word. Listen for the vowel sound you hear in **saw**.

Think and Sort

All of the spelling words have the vowel sound in **saw**. Spell each word aloud.

Look at the letters in each word. Think about how the vowel sound in **saw** is spelled.

1. Write the two spelling words that have **aw**.
2. Write the six spelling words that have **a**.
3. Write the six spelling words that have **o**.

Use the steps on page iv to study words that are hard for you.

Spelling Patterns

The vowel sound in **saw** can be spelled **aw**, **a**, or **o**.

aw	a	o
saw	ball	dog

Name ______________________ Date ____________

Spelling and Meaning

Word Groups Write the spelling word that belongs in each group.

1. pup, hound, ____________ **2.** yell, shout, ____________

3. tadpole, toad, ____________ **4.** run, jog, ____________

5. speak, say, ____________

6. paint, sketch, ____________

7. looked, watched, ____________

8. music, tune, ____________

Antonyms Antonyms are words that have opposite meanings. Complete each sentence by writing the spelling word that is an antonym of the word in dark type.

9. The room was very ____________. **large**

10. Have you ____________ your red hat? **found**

11. Last year her hair was ____________. **short**

12. Please turn ____________ the light. **on**

13. We found ____________ of the missing screws. **none**

Word Story Many years ago in England, a round object used in sports was called a **beall**. The spelling of **beall** has changed only a little. Write the spelling that we use today.

14. ____________________

Family Tree: call Think about how the **call** words are alike in spelling and meaning. Then add another **call** word to the tree.

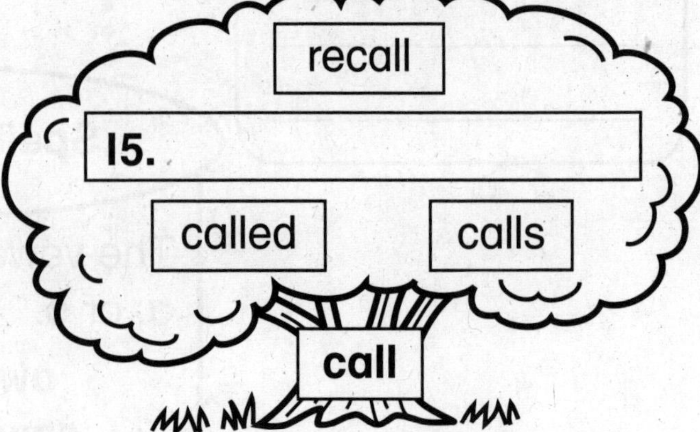

Name ______________________ Date ____________

Spelling in Context

Use each spelling word once to complete the story.

Harvey, the Pet That Wasn't

Last summer all my friends could ______(1) about was their pets. Taylor's ______(2) had learned to roll over. Jack's fish tank was too full. I had to paint or ______(3) pictures of animals. I had no pet of my own.

I had wanted a pet for a ______(4) time. But my parents don't like furry animals. Dogs and cats make my brother sneeze. I did have a little turtle once. One day it ran away and got ______(5). Then Dad said I could get a fish. A fish wasn't exciting to me. You can't take a fish for a ______(6). A fish won't chase a ______(7). But a fish is better than nothing. Jack said he had a perfect fish for me. My fish was ______(8), but it had big eyes. I named it Harvey.

It didn't take me long to figure out that Harvey wasn't a fish at ______(9).

Name ______________________ Date ____________

When I ______________ little legs start to grow from his sides, I knew I was in trouble!

10

I could not believe my eyes. I had an about-to-be ______________! What would my parents say if they saw a frog hopping down the hall? What would happen when they heard Harvey singing that well-known frog ______________, "Ribbit, Ribbit"?

11

12

I took my little tadpole to the pond. I watched him swim ______________ to find some friends.

13

I'm not going to ______________ Jack for a while. Not until I have thought of a way to pay him back for his little joke!

14

- saw
- song
- talk
- dog
- call
- frog
- off
- ball
- draw
- all
- lost
- small
- walk
- long

★ Challenge Yourself ★

Challenge Words

false
haul
faucet

Use a dictionary to answer these questions. Then use the Challenge Words to write sentences on separate paper.

15. Will people trust you if you say things that are **false**? ______________

16. Can a truck **haul** branches to another place? ______________

17. Could you find a **faucet** in a kitchen? ______________

Name ______________________ Date ____________

Lesson 28: The Vowel Sound in *for*

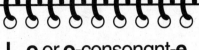

horse

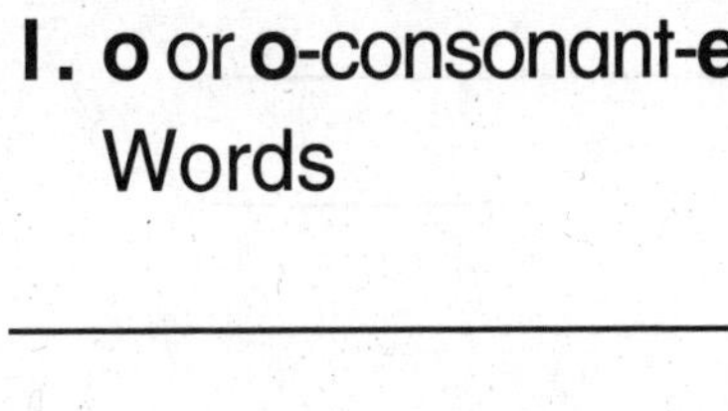

1. o or **o**-consonant-**e** Words

____

____

____

____

____

____

____

____

____

____

____

2. oo Words

____

____

3. ou Word

____

for
corn
door
or
story
short
snore
more
horse
storm
four
orange
floor
store

Say and Listen

Say each spelling word. Listen for the vowel sound you hear in **for**.

Think and Sort

All of the spelling words have the vowel sound in **for**. Spell each word aloud.

Look at the letters in each word. Think about how the vowel sound in **for** is spelled.

1. Write the eleven spelling words that have **o** or **o**-consonant-**e**.
2. Write the two spelling words that have **oo**.
3. Write the one spelling word that has **ou**.

Use the steps on page iv to study words that are hard for you.

Spelling Patterns

The vowel sound in **for** can be spelled **o**, **o**-consonant-**e**, **oo**, or **ou**.

o	**o**-consonant-**e**	**oo**	**ou**
for	more	door	four

Name ________________________ Date ____________

Spelling and Meaning

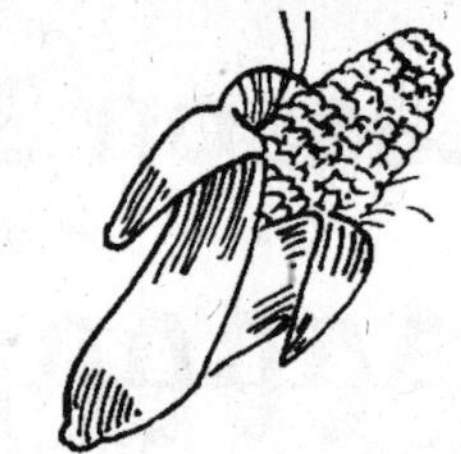

Word Meanings Write the spelling word for each meaning. Use a dictionary if you need to.

1. a yellow grain ____________
2. very bad weather ____________
3. a place where goods are sold ____________
4. not tall ____________
5. the number after three ____________
6. a large four-legged animal with hooves ____________

Clues Write the spelling word for each clue.

7. You want this if you want extra. ____________
8. This word is used on a gift card. ____________
9. This word can join two others. ____________
10. You can drink this juice for breakfast. ____________
11. Some people do this when they sleep. ____________
12. You go in and out through this. ____________
13. People walk on this. ____________

Word Story One of the spelling words means "a tale." It comes from the Old French word **estorie**. In Old English it was spelled **storie**. The spelling changed over time, and **ie** became **y**. Write the spelling that we use today.

14. ____________

Family Tree: short Think about how the **short** words are alike in spelling and meaning. Then add another **short** word to the tree.

Name ______________________________ Date ____________

Spelling in Context

Use each spelling word once to complete the story.

Rainy Day Recipe

It was raining outside. "What can we do?" Joey asked Rita. "If we had some money, we could go to the ______________."
1

"But we don't have any money," she said. "You could tell me a scary ______________."
2

"Oh, no! I don't know any stories. Let's go down to Uncle Burt's until this awful ______________ is over."
3

Uncle Burt lived on the ______________ just below theirs. They
4
locked the ______________ to their apartment and took the
5
______________ elevator ride to Uncle Burt's.
6

Uncle Burt and Scooter were in the kitchen. Scooter was a Saint Bernard. He was almost as big as a ______________!
7
Most Saint Bernards are brown and white. Scooter was ______________ and white. Scooter was asleep. Now and then
8
he would ______________, growl, ______________ bark in
9 10
his sleep.

"I'm going to make meat loaf ______________ supper," said
11
Uncle Burt. "You can read the list of what we need, Joey."

Name ______________________ Date __________

Joey read out loud from the cookbook:

"Two pounds of hamburger, one cup of bread crumbs, one small can of ________ (12), one cup of grated cheese, and one chopped onion."

Uncle Burt started to cut up the onion. The onion made him cry. He rubbed his eyes. That made him cry even ________ (13). He had to stop for ________ (14) or five minutes.

Rita put everything in a bowl. Everyone took a turn at mixing. Then they put the meat loaf in the oven. When the storm stopped, the meat loaf was ready.

"How do you like that, Scooter?" Joey asked.

"Woof!" barked Scooter.

for
corn
door
or
story
short
snore
more
horse
storm
four
orange
floor
store

★ Challenge Yourself ★

Challenge Words

torch
organ
orchard

Use a dictionary to answer these questions. Then use the Challenge Words to write sentences on separate paper.

15. Does a **torch** give off light? ________

16. Could you play an **organ** while marching in a band? ________

17. Could you find apples in an **orchard**? ________

Name ______________________ Date ____________

Lesson 29: The Vowel Sound in *jar*

car

1. a Word

____

2. ar Words

____

____

____

____

____

____

____

____

____

____

____

____

____

jar
car
party
barn
arm
father
mark
farmer
star
are
dark
farm
far
art

Say and Listen

Say each spelling word. Listen for the vowel sound you hear in **jar**.

Think and Sort

All of the spelling words have the vowel sound in **jar**. The sound is spelled **a** in each word. Look at the letters in each word. Spell each word aloud.

1. Write the one spelling word that has **a**.
2. Write the thirteen spelling words that have **ar**.

Use the steps on page iv to study words that are hard for you.

Spelling Patterns

The vowel sound in **jar** can be spelled **a**.

f**a**ther	j**a**r

Name ______________________ Date ____________

Spelling and Meaning

Word Groups Write the spelling word that belongs in each group.

1. gardener, rancher, ______________
2. music, reading, ______________
3. hand, wrist, ______________
4. glass, bottle, ______________
5. is, am, ______________
6. garden, ranch, ______________
7. brother, mother, ______________
8. black, unlit, ______________

Rhymes Write the spelling word that completes each sentence and rhymes with the underlined word.

9. You traveled ______________ in your <u>car</u>.
10. Did <u>Marty</u> go to the ______________?
11. The <u>shark</u> had a ______________ on its fin.
12. How <u>far</u> away is that ______________?
13. The cat carried the <u>yarn</u> to the ______________.

Word Story One spelling word once was a name for a wagon. Some people spelled it **carrus**. Today the spelling word is another word for **automobile**. Write the word.

14. ______________

Family Tree: farm Think about how the **farm** words are alike in spelling and meaning. Then add another **farm** word to the tree.

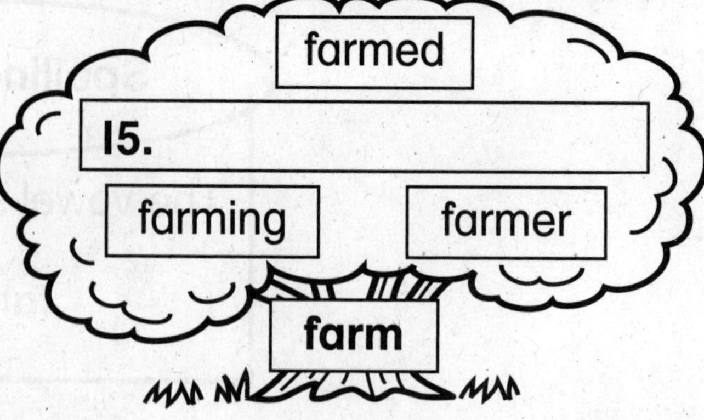

Name ______________________ Date ____________

Spelling in Context

Use each spelling word once to complete the story.

The Star Party

Four children lived with their parents and grandmother on a pretty ________ (1). The ________ (2) and his wife worked hard. They had a ________ (3) full of animals to take care of every day.

One summer night the grandmother looked up at the sky. "My eyes are bad," she said sadly. "I can't see a single ________ (4) anymore."

That night after dinner, the mother and ________ (5) took the children for a ride in the ________ (6). They made a plan to make the grandmother happy.

The next night the father said, "Tonight we are having a star ________ (7). The presents ________ (8) all ready. Let the party begin!"

The first child gave the grandmother a kitten. It had a white ________ (9) on its face just like a star. The second child had made a bracelet of yellow stars. The grandmother put it on her ________ (10). The third child had

Name ______________________ Date ____________

covered the garden with a hundred stars cut from silver paper. The garden was a work of ______________.
11

Then the youngest child quietly handed the grandmother a glass ______________ with a lid. He told her to open the jar outside.
12

The grandmother went out to the garden and took the lid off the jar. Everyone smiled. Fireflies flew all around. They glowed brightly in the ______________.
13

"It's a jar of stars!" said the youngest child.

The grandmother said, "I love the stars you gave me. Now I don't need to see the stars that are so ______________ away."
14

- jar
- car
- party
- barn
- arm
- father
- mark
- farmer
- star
- are
- dark
- farm
- far
- art

★ Challenge Yourself ★

Challenge Words

barber
depart
harmful

Write the Challenge Word for each clue. Check a dictionary to see if you are right. Then use the Challenge Words to write sentences on separate paper.

15. You do this when you leave for school. ______________

16. Something that hurts you is this. ______________

17. This person cuts hair. ______________

Name ______________________ Date __________

Lesson 30: Words with *er*

painter

1. No Change to Base Word

____
____
____
____
____
____
____

2. Final Consonant Doubled

____
____
____
____

3. Final **e** Dropped

____
____
____

colder
bigger
helper
shopper
braver
runner
writer
older
longer
jumper
flatter
faster
painter
baker

Say and Listen

Say each spelling word. Listen for the ending sounds.

Think and Sort

Each spelling word is made by adding **er** to a base word. In which spelling words does the spelling of the base word change?

1. Write the seven spelling words with no change in the base word.

2. Write the four spelling words in which the final consonant of the base word is doubled.

3. Write the three spelling words in which the final **e** of the base word is dropped.

Use the steps on page iv to study words that are hard for you.

Spelling Patterns

No Change to Base Word	Final Consonant Doubled	Final **e** Dropped
colder	**flatt**er	**brav**er

Name ______________________________ Date ______________

Spelling and Meaning

Word Meanings Write the spelling word for each meaning.

1. someone who shops ______________
2. someone who helps ______________
3. someone who writes stories ______________
4. more able to face danger ______________
5. someone who runs ______________
6. more flat ______________
7. someone who jumps ______________
8. one who colors things ______________

Antonyms Antonyms are words that have opposite meanings. Complete each sentence by writing the spelling word that is an antonym of the word in dark type.

9. Kay is ______________ than her sister. **younger**
10. The turtle was ______________ than the rabbit. **slower**
11. My legs are ______________ than yours. **shorter**
12. Jesse's feet are ______________ than mine. **smaller**
13. The night was ______________ than the day. **hotter**

Word Story Back in the year 800, the Old English word **bacan** meant "to bake." Later, a person who baked was called a **baecere**. Write the spelling for **baecere** that we use today.

14. ______________

Family Tree: help Think about how the **help** words are alike in spelling and meaning. Then add another **help** word to the tree.

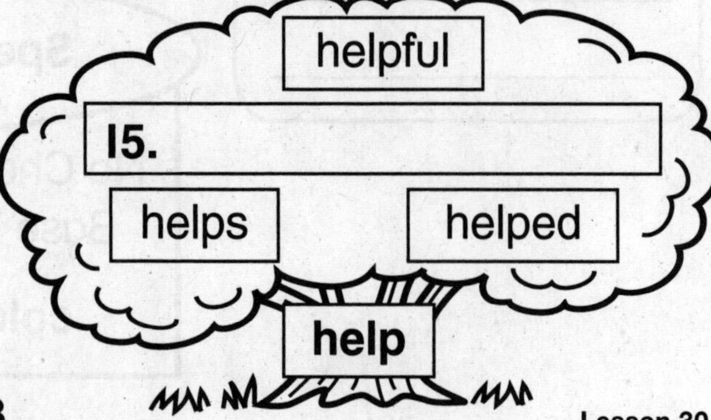